Praise for *The Listening*

'I wholeheartedly suppo   ep
relevance to our lives ar   ur
world.'

Nancy Kline, best-selling author of *Time to Think*

'Tamsin Hartley shows you how to create a gently powerful listening space by combining mindfulness and metaphor through the medium of Clean Language. Extremely readable, with some great examples of how real people deal with gritty real-life problems by offering themselves and those they live and work with the simple, spacious, lucid clarity of The Listening Space.'

Nick Pole, author of *Words That Touch*

'A beautifully crafted book which takes you on a journey of personal discovery through the Lighthouse of Mindful Exploration. Inside we learn how to listen to both ourselves and to others without judgement. I felt supported all the way through the book, as though the author was right next to me, guiding me through a series of short and enjoyable activities that helped me to develop the skills needed to create a Listening Space for others. This practical handbook is full of interesting anecdotes, examples, activities and tips. It is very easy to read and is likely to significantly improve your listening skills and your ability to provide a truly resourceful space for someone to hear and explore their own thinking.'

Sue Sharp, Coach and Trainer, *Your Emerging Self*

'*The Listening Space: A New Path to Personal Discovery* is the first work to combine the art of mindfulness with metaphor and David Grove's Clean Language questions. It shows how paying mindful attention to yourself and others results in more awareness, more acceptance, less judgment and more choice. Although written for beginners starting on their path of personal discovery, *The Listening Space* has plenty for more experienced seekers, and for the professionals who work with them. The unique way this book combines mindfulness and Clean Language will give you new and exciting ways to know yourself and to experience the world around you.'

Penny Tompkins and James Lawley,
authors of *Metaphors in Mind*

'An eminently practical and readable book with a comprehensive range of development tools and exercises, leading to an innovative and streamlined process that will amplify your listening awareness in a non-judgemental way, allowing people to discover their own unique personal solutions. This is a 'must-have' book for your bookshelf. One that you will come back to and discover new and refreshing insights.'

John Gallagher, Hypnotherapist/NLP Practitioner,
Life's Purpose

'This empowering book demonstrates clearly and simply how awareness of your own personal metaphors can influence your behaviour and change your life for the better.'

A.C., primary school teacher

'Desperate to improve communication with my three teenagers, I found *The Listening Space* really helped me with that and much more! This cleverly written book provides a clear explanation of the concept of Clean Language by taking the reader on a path into and up through the different floors of a Lighthouse of Mindful Exploration. At each stage the book reinforces the theory by suggesting exercises and techniques which are easy to follow and helped me to start using Clean questions straight away! What started for me as a tool to improve communication has become a powerful resource which has encouraged me to step back and explore my own thoughts and emotions too. A real gem and one to keep by your bedside!'

J.M., parent

The
Listening Space

A New Path to Personal Discovery

Tamsin Hartley

For John.

Contents

Preface to the Second Edition

The Listening Space is a unique and structured way of listening that has had a transformative effect on the lives of many.

In the three years since the publication of the first edition of this book, this listening process has been refined and simplified in the light of feedback from people who have been using The Listening Space in their everyday lives.

It is now easier to learn and continues to produce surprising and profoundly creative insights for the people being listened to.

Whilst much of the book remains the same, Chapter 4 of this revised edition has been significantly updated to reflect these changes.

Introduction

What drew you to this book?

Perhaps you were curious about the mention of **The Listening Space** in the title? So many of us find ourselves caught up in the busy demands of life. We rush from one commitment to another, trying to fit too much into each day with barely a moment to catch our breath. It can feel like we're being pulled in all directions with no time to stop and enjoy life. We get caught up in our thoughts and emotions, 'trapped' in reliving past problems or worrying about future events. We can find ourselves struggling to make decisions and being uncertain about the direction we want to take. We don't stop for a moment to listen... truly listen to ourselves and others. Maybe there have been times when you have felt pressurised in this way?

This book will give you simple tools to help you pause for breath, slow time down and create space to listen to yourself and others. These tools are based on the principles of mindfulness. You will be invited to:

- pay non-judgemental attention to your physical body;
- become an observer of your thoughts and emotions rather than getting swept up in the usual emotional responses you have to what is happening; and
- develop an awareness of all the preconceptions that you bring to your experiences and interactions with others.

You will be encouraged to live in the richness of each unfolding moment and connect with what feels right to you in the choices that you make. Some of these tools of mindful exploration you can use on yourself. Others you can use with someone else who is learning these skills as you create a space to listen to one another. Either way, you will discover more about yourself.

You can also use these tools to discover more about how others are experiencing their lives so that you can understand them better and avoid or overcome misunderstandings. You might use them with a family member, colleague or friend: to get to the bottom of what is bothering your child; to communicate more constructively with your partner; to understand where colleagues or people from other disciplines are coming from. If your work involves dealing with customers, clients or patients, you might use these tools to become clearer about how you can best be of service to them.

What Do We Mean by Mindful Exploration?

Mindful exploration is about getting to know ourselves better as we bring our attention to what is going on both inside and around us in the present moment. It is about allowing ourselves to experience the whole range of our thoughts and emotions – from pure joy to painful vulnerability – and accepting our responses to what is happening in our lives. This is not to say that we have to accept the situation itself. Suppose, for example, that I am angry and frustrated with the way that my manager is treating me. Whilst I might accept that these are my feelings, this does not mean that I must accept that person's actions.

Developing awareness of this kind helps us to see each moment as it unfolds around us with more clarity. It enables us to respond to what is actually happening rather than reacting to situations with all the worries and concerns from past events or imagined future happenings. Choices and solutions that were previously hidden from view are given the chance to reveal themselves.

This subtle shift can have a profound, positive impact on our ability to cope with the pressures of life. Everywhere we turn nowadays there are accounts of how developing a practice of mindful awareness is helping to contribute to people's emotional wellbeing in a variety of different ways:

- Reducing levels of anxiety and/or depression.
- Improving concentration and thinking ability.
- Increasing our ability to be more empathic and compassionate towards others.

What Do We Mean by Emotional Wellbeing?

Emotional wellbeing refers to our ability to manage our state of mind so that we can deal with the stresses and strains of daily life in a constructive way. Most of us know only too well how quickly our mental or emotional state can change from one moment to the next – spending time with a good friend can lift our spirits and make anything seem possible, whereas hearing bad news makes even the simplest of tasks difficult to focus on.

People often think about wellbeing in terms of the things they have: their job, home, family and friends. In fact, it is the way we think that has the biggest impact on our wellbeing, because the way we think determines the way we respond to what is happening in our lives. If, for example, I believe that I am worthy of love and belonging, I am likely to be more resilient to life's inevitable setbacks. However, if I believe that I am not worthy or deserving in some way, then I am likely to lean towards more catastrophic thinking when things go wrong.

Mindful exploration helps us to see more clearly how our thoughts and emotions drive the way that we react to the world around us and consequently determine the choices we make. We open our eyes to more resourceful ways of experiencing and responding to the present moment.

Our emotional wellbeing lies at the heart of our ability to live life with a sense of meaning and purpose. It enables us to value and accept ourselves so that we can:

- deal with times of uncertainty and change;
- build positive relationships with other people;
- live and work productively; and
- engage with the world and contribute to the community around us.

Perhaps, on the other hand, you were drawn to this book because you were intrigued by the mention of a **New Path to Personal Discovery** in the book's title? This new path is about taking a different approach to mindful exploration as you create space to connect with the choices that are right for you. There is nothing new about mindfulness itself – indeed, it is a very ancient practice. However, in this book you will be taught new ways of understanding yourself as you uncover the **metaphors** that you naturally use to describe your experience.

Why Metaphor?

Metaphors describe one thing in terms of another and give form to things which are otherwise difficult to describe. Take, for example, a friend who recently explained that, for her, trying to stay in control was creating a '*tension all around the top half of my body, like big iron armour crushing inwards.*' We get a very graphic sense of how this person was experiencing her situation from the metaphor she used.

Metaphors are not simply a figure of speech; they play a fundamental role in the way we understand ourselves and the world around us. It seems that we actually structure our thinking through metaphor, although we are not usually consciously aware of doing so. When we shine a light on the metaphors that we naturally use to describe our experience we often reveal a richness of information that would otherwise have remained hidden. These metaphors can be an almost magical way of getting to know ourselves better.

The Lighthouse of Mindful Exploration

This brings us to the purpose of this book. In this book you will:

- be shown ways of becoming **mindful** of the present moment by tuning in to your different senses, your thoughts and your emotions;
- be encouraged to access your own **metaphors** to describe your experiences and bring your

self-exploration to a whole new colourful and creative level; and

- learn how to create a **Listening Space** for others to explore their own experience, which may or may not be through metaphor.

I have my own metaphor for the way that the book is structured – that of a **Lighthouse of Mindful Exploration**. This lighthouse stands tall on the rocks by the sea. It is accessed by climbing three shallow steps to a varnished wooden door. This door is unlocked easily by using the wrought iron **Key of Curiosity** that hangs on a hook to the right of the handle.

All are welcome to enter and explore. However, before doing so we must wipe our feet on the **Welcome Mat** on the top step so that we can remove any desire to fix or make better. There is no place for offering advice or solutions in this building.

We will also need to understand a little about the fabric of the building before entering – the **Clean Bricks** from which the building is made. These bricks are made of **Clean Language**, a specific set of questions that help people to explore their thinking in their own way. We will learn how asking questions of people in this way leaves them free to explore their thinking without contamination from our own assumptions and suggestions. These bricks are what makes the lighthouse so robust and dependable, and so very enlightening.

We will then be ready to step over the threshold into the ground floor room, but I'm going to press pause and explain a little more about Clean Language before I tell you about the rest of our journey through the lighthouse.

What Is Clean Language?

Clean Language is a simple, powerful and respectful way of communicating, of exploring a situation, and of facilitating change. At its heart lies a specific set of questions (called Clean questions) that help to keep the assumptions, suggestions and interpretations of the person asking the questions (**the facilitator**) out of the way. This leaves the person answering the questions (who we will call **the explorer** in this book) free to do their own thinking about their situation.

Clean questions can be used to focus on the metaphors that people use to express themselves. When this happens people experience being listened to at a very deep level and can be facilitated to make transformative and long-lasting changes.

What Kind of Questions Are Clean Questions?

Clean questions are a specific set of simple questions. The rules for using them are straightforward – use only the words or phrases that the explorer has used along with a Clean question. This means that the facilitator must listen with very careful attention to what the explorer is saying.

The two most commonly-used questions are:

> **What kind of** 'x'?
> **Is there anything else about** 'x'?
> (where 'x' is a word or phrase that the other person has used)

Throughout the book I'll be highlighting the Clean questions by putting them in bold.

Let's take a look at an example of these two questions being asked during a conversation between an employee and her manager:

Employee: *I'm stuck with writing this report.*
Manager: **What kind of** stuck is that?
Employee: *Well I'm not sure how to structure the recommendations section.*
Manager: **Is there anything else about** that structure?
Employee: *Yes. I don't think I'm really clear about what the stakeholders are looking for. I guess I need to ask them. Once I've clarified that I'll know what needs to be included.*

In this instance, with just two questions the employee has found her own solution to her situation.

How Can Clean Questions Be Used?

The previous example shows how Clean questions can be used to clarify ideas and help people to solve problems or make good decisions. They can also be used to:

- clear up or avoid misconceptions;
- clarify desired outcomes;
- motivate people to take action; and
- uncover the structure (or mental model) of someone's thinking.

Perhaps, for example, there is someone you know who is particularly good at managing his or her team. Clean questions would be an ideal tool for finding out more about that person's mental model for doing this – in other words, the way they are thinking. Maybe they see themselves as the conductor of an orchestra, making sure that everyone is playing the same symphony and that each instrument is ready to play on cue. These questions help you keep your own assumptions tucked well away as you invite them to explore their thinking further. Likely as not, they will reveal a richness of information that would not have seen the light of day if you'd jumped in with your comments, suggestions or advice.

This approach can be used to explore any aspect of a person's personal or work life: from writing reports, to managing time, to the way they deal with stress in their life. By asking Clean questions it is possible to unpick:

- what's working well; and
- what's not working so well.

The insights gained from exploring things in this way frequently result in greater clarity about what would work better for them instead.

So, let us return to our tour of the Lighthouse of Mindful Exploration.

After opening the door with the Key of Curiosity and wiping our feet on the Welcome Mat (to remove any desire to fix or solve), we are now ready to enter the warm and welcoming open space that is the ground floor room. This room is about **Being With Yourself**. Scattered on the floor in front of us lie seven big, brightly-coloured beanbag cushions – each a different colour of the rainbow. We will visit each beanbag in turn to tune in to the different aspects of awareness that they represent: our five senses, our thoughts and our emotions.

As we bring our awareness to the stream of thoughts that we experience we will notice how they come and go, rather like clouds passing in the sky. The activities in this room will invite us to hold painful thoughts and feelings in balanced awareness rather than over-identifying with them. It can be very liberating to realise that our thoughts are simply 'mental events' that do not have to control us.

Having spent some time tuning in to our own experience, it will be time to climb the stairs that lead us through a gap in the ceiling to the first floor, **The Metaphor Room**, where we will learn more about the fundamental role metaphor plays in our thinking. We will discover how asking Clean questions of the metaphors that we naturally use helps us to bring them into focus, making them more defined and tangible. These metaphors can be both powerfully revealing and richly creative. For example, there were times when I felt over-whelmed by the task of writing this book. A friend used Clean questions to help me explore this feeling and before long a metaphor appeared. Writing each chapter was like climbing the tall sand dunes on Bamburgh Beach. The harder I tried to get to the top, the more I sank into the sand. I realised that I needed to go at a slow and steady pace, focussing on one step at a time. It was important to pause every now and again and turn around to enjoy the view out to sea. I could also make sure I had fun on the run down before embarking on the next chapter's climb.

Our exploration so far has focused on shining a **Clean Light of Attention** on ourselves. It is important to spend time getting to know yourself better before taking the stairs up to the second floor of the lighthouse, where you will be invited to apply what you have learnt so far to create a Listening Space for others. On this floor, **Being With Others**, you will be encouraged to have a partner in exploration. Together you will experience both asking and being asked Clean questions to explore your current experience in a way that encourages metaphors to reveal themselves. Not only will you get the benefit of being an explorer, you will also experience the privilege of being witness to another person's exploration in this way.

At this point I ought to explain that a Listening Space should not be confused with counselling, coaching or therapy. It is a structured process that can be used by anyone and is about creating a safe space for a person to explore his or her thinking.

Finally, we will climb up to the very top of the building, **The Lantern Room**, where we will consider how we can take what has been learnt in our journey up the building out into our everyday lives. We will look at situations where Clean exploration – using Clean questions to shine the light of attention on ourselves and others – can help to:

- gain clarity on which direction to take next;
- navigate the rocks and storms in life; and
- notice the beauty in the surrounding landscape.

We will be introduced to seven individuals from very different walks of life. Each have their stories to tell about the impact that Clean exploration has had for them.

The Structure of the Book
This book will take you step by step, floor by floor, from the doorstep to the top of the building, with a chapter to parallel each stage of the journey:

Chapter 1: Entering the Building
Chapter 2: Being With Yourself
Chapter 3: The Metaphor Room
Chapter 4: Being With Others
Chapter 5: The Lantern Room

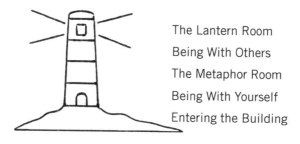

The Lantern Room

Being With Others

The Metaphor Room

Being With Yourself

Entering the Building

How you read the book will depend on your interests and experience. However, if you are new to the ideas in the book, I would encourage you to follow the sections in the order that we climb our way through the lighthouse.

I will be suggesting activities for you to do throughout the book, which are an integral part of the learning. Some of the activities can be done alone, whilst others will involve a partner. The shared activities will let you know how it feels both to facilitate and be facilitated with the various questions. It is only by doing these activities that you will get a true sense of what happens for you when you develop mindful awareness through your own metaphors.

What You Will Gain From Reading This Book

Joining me on the tour of this lighthouse will enable you to explore your experience and listen to yourself better as you:

- pay non-judgemental attention to your physical body;
- become an observer of your thoughts and emotions rather than getting swept up in the usual emotional responses you have to what is happening; and

- discover metaphors that capture your experience in a way that is unique to you.

The result of this exploration will be that you:

- become more aware of how you are living your life;
- come to know what feels right for you in the decisions you make;
- become clearer about the directions you want to take in life; and
- feel more at ease with yourself and have more enjoyment in what you do.

The tools that you learn in this book will also enable you to listen to others differently, helping you to understand them better and connect with them in richer, more fulfilling ways.

I hope you enjoy the tour.

Chapter 1

Entering the Building

Life is a journey to be experienced, not a problem to be solved.

A.A. Milne

It's time to climb the steps to the **Lighthouse of Mindful Exploration** and start our journey through the building, where we will explore different ways of coming to know ourselves better. But there are three things we must do before entering to ensure that we bring with us a mindset of open-minded curiosity:

- Wipe our feet on the **Welcome Mat** and, in so doing, wipe away any desire to analyse, judge or fix.
- Use the **Key of Curiosity** to unlock the door.
- Notice the **Clean Bricks** from which the building is constructed.

You may be wondering why we need to resist the temptation to make things better when it is human nature to want to find solutions to our problems. To answer this question we first need to understand why having a safe space to explore the whole range of our thoughts and emotions is so important when it comes to our mental and emotional wellbeing.

1. The Welcome Mat

It may come as a surprise to you to know that feeling good about ourselves isn't just about feeling happy and positive. A successful life, a good job, a nice home – none of these things guarantee us feelings of self-worth. We've all heard stories of celebrity millionaires who live a troubled existence in spite of all their wealth and popularity. Equally there are people who are very contented leading simple, non-materialistic lives.

In fact, it seems the thing that most influences our feelings of self-worth is our relationship with vulnerability. In her fascinating research on shame and vulnerability, Brené Brown discovered that people who feel worthy have one thing in common: they believe that although being vulnerable is uncomfortable, it is a necessary part of life. These people are able to wake up in the morning and think, *'No matter what gets done and how much is left undone, I am enough.'* They are able to go to bed at night thinking, *'Yes, I am imperfect and vulnerable and sometimes afraid, but that doesn't change the truth that I am also brave and worthy of love and belonging.'* She calls this **living wholeheartedly**.[1]

1. Brown, B. (2010). *The Gifts of Imperfection: Let Go of Who You Think You're Supposed to Be and Embrace Who You Are.* Minnesota: Hazelden Publishing.

For these people, vulnerability is not something to be feared or avoided. Rather, it is just part of what it means to be human. There is no 'if and **when** list' to feeling worthy:

*I'll be good enough **when** I'm thinner/fitter/*
  more accomplished.
*I'd be good enough **if** I were smarter/more attractive/*
  more sociable.

For most of us, however, vulnerability makes us fear that we are in some way 'not enough' – that we're not smart enough/ not attractive enough/not sociable enough/that our children aren't accomplished enough – the list goes on. You could say that we live in a culture of scarcity, of 'never enough' (or so the media would have us believe). Messages all around us fuel that 'if only' voice in our head:

If only I were thinner/funnier/fitter.
If only he'd try harder/didn't try so hard.
If only the organisation was more compassionate/
  more competitive.
If only I didn't have dyslexia/heart disease/cancer.

Sounding familiar? Advertising depends on it, telling us how things would be so much better for us 'if only' we had this latest product or made that particular lifestyle choice.

Fuelled by vulnerability, shame lurks pervasively in the shadows, reminding us of all the ways to believe that we are 'not enough'. It drains us of the energy and courage to take action where there are no guarantees of success:

Don't apply for that job because you're not smart enough.
Don't ask her out because you're not attractive enough.
Don't leave him because you're not strong enough
  without him.

Shame contaminates the way we think about ourselves and the world around us. Those 'not enough' messages keep popping up uninvited in the in-box of our thoughts:

Remember, you're not brave/bright/beautiful enough!

Over time these messages become embedded in our thinking, installed like programmes running in the background on a computer. We build our 'not enough' beliefs up over the course of a lifetime. As children we are particularly susceptible to them. Without the benefit of perspective that experience brings, we take the things that the adults around us say as truths. And whilst some of these 'truths' are empowering, many are not.

We hear things like:

> *You're lazy.*

> *You're not very considerate.*

When it would be more accurate to say:

> *I think you could have done more work on that project.*

> *I don't think that was a very considerate thing to do.*

We unwittingly build our identity around these 'truths' and convince ourselves that this is who we are:

> I **am** inconsiderate.
> I **am** lazy.

These shame 'belief programmes' have a powerful impact on the decisions we make and the actions we take (or choose not to take). They make us tend to catastrophise in our thinking about situations – to imagine the worst that will happen. We get swept up in emotional responses that are often based on more negative, paranoid thinking, rather than pausing to see what is actually happening and taking a more balanced perspective.

Ironically, we can also feel vulnerable when things are going well for us: when we are feeling joyful, fulfilled or content; when we are doing well in our job; when we are feeling vital and healthy. We fear the loss of these good things since we believe they cannot last.

It is worth remembering, however, that whilst vulnerability can be excruciating, it also lies at the heart of meaningful human experience. It is often in moments when we allow our true, precious and vulnerable selves to be seen that we are most connected to others.

Armouring Up

Since feeling vulnerable does not come high on most people's wish list, most of us will do anything to protect ourselves against it – and we have some pretty impressive methods of protection at our disposal!

We might don our **Flak Jacket of Perfection** to fend off criticism and hope that we won't be discovered for who we really are. Instead we pretend to be the person we feel we 'ought to be', whatever that might mean for us: be strong, always put others before yourself, always try hard, never let others down. We say to ourselves things like:

If I'm perfect, if I achieve all this, if I'm better than the rest, then I can't be criticised.
If I hide my imperfections inside this jacket, then nobody needs to know that they exist.

We may hold up our **Shield of Safety** to keep vulnerability at a safe distance – our barrier to engaging in relationships with others that protects us from rejection and loss. We hold back from commitment to business or personal projects to keep failure at bay, and ensure that we have an exit strategy ready to pull us out at the earliest sign of difficulty.

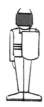

And finally, on our head we may wear our protective helmet with its **Visor of Certainty**, which shows us how the world 'ought to be'. It convinces us that the way we see things is the 'right way' – depending on our past experiences, our upbringing and cultural background. It reassures us that there is right and wrong, good and bad, and predictability in what we see. When we are confronted by information from our senses that contradicts our beliefs or values we feel uncomfortable and strive for consistency to relieve the discomfort. The visor acts as a filter, deleting or distorting the information from our eyes that doesn't fit with our mental model of how the world works, so leaving our beliefs and values intact. With our visor down we defend ourselves with dogma so that we don't need to face the ambiguities and shades of grey that are an inherent part of life.

The phrases on the following page are the kinds of things we might say when our visors are firmly down.

> My religious/political/ personal beliefs are the right ones.

> This is good behaviour – that is bad.

> This is the right way to be a parent – that way is wrong.

Equally, the helmet filters the sound that enters our ears. We hear the opinions that we think are 'valid' and don't hear the rest. For example, some people will only hear praise and others only criticism.

Most of us are not consciously aware of the protection that we have put in place. And, unfortunately, our armour is never fully bulletproof – failure, criticism and disappointment will always find a way of seeping in through the gaps in our defences. However much we try to create a safety zone of predictability around us we cannot control life. Life is uncertain – there are no guarantees.

Our armour only serves to stop us being true to ourselves and drives disconnection from others:

- Our **Flak-Jacket of Perfection** fuels self-blame and crippling inaction lest we should fall short of the mark.
- Our **Shield of Safety** keeps all emotions at arm's length. We not only guard ourselves against vulnerability, but also from happiness, joy, love and creativity.
- Our **Visor of Certainty** restricts us from seeing different perspectives. It fuels one-upmanship and criticism. We foster the illusion of control and

certainty at the cost of meaningful connection with others.

There are times when our armour is appropriate – for example, in the various professional roles where being strong and capable is required. And there may be times when we need to arm ourselves to keep ourselves safe – such as when we are with people who want to manipulate us for their advantage. However, our protection can clearly create its own problems, and if we want to nurture our sense of self-worth we need to have the opportunity to remove it in safety so that we can embrace our vulnerability.

Embracing Vulnerability

When we take off our Visor of Certainty, hang up our Flak Jacket of Perfection and put down our Shield of Safety, we open our senses to what is actually happening for us. At times this will mean facing up to feelings that are deeply uncomfortable – those 'monsters in the cupboard' that sit in the recesses of our minds. It's tempting to just want to box these monsters away, shut the lid on them (firmly) and walk away. But if we want to live with a sense of self-worth, of love and belonging, we're going to have to roll up our sleeves and lean into the discomfort of ambiguity and uncertainty. We can't selectively filter out the thoughts and emotions that don't fit with the stories we create for who we would like to be: the high-flying student, the supportive partner, the nurturing parent, the capable employee, the accomplished artist.

Fortunately, it seems that shame is not the hardy creature we might think it is. It withers when we have a safe space where we can talk in an uncensored way, where we will be listened to without interruption, where we will not be judged, where we can talk without someone trying to 'fix' us and make us a 'better person', and where we know that what we say will not become the topic of next week's gossip. In this space we can learn to accept who we actually are rather than pretending to be someone we are not. This is the kind of space which destroys shame and where a sense of self-worth and belonging grows – whether we are listening to ourselves, listening to others or having others listen to us.

With a growing sense of self-worth we risk doing things where there are no guarantees, we risk investing in relationships or projects that may not work out. And when mistakes do happen we shift from pointing the finger of blame at ourselves or others to seeing what we can learn from the experience. When we make poor choices we say to ourselves, *What I did was wrong*, rather than listening to the voice of shame that says, *I am a bad person because I did this*.

So, before you enter the building, wipe your feet on the Welcome Mat, leave judgement and a desire to fix at the door, and step into the building with the courage to embrace your vulnerability – because vulnerability is also the place where joy, creativity, love and connection can grow. Open your heart to being the person that you already are – warts, weakness and all!

2. The Key of Curiosity

A mindset of curiosity is probably the single most important component to opening the door to compassionate and wholehearted exploration of our own experience and the experience of others. In this building we will set the intention of setting aside our assumptions about how things 'ought' to be so that we can enquire with open-minded fascination about how things actually are. The tool we will be using to help us do this lies in the very fabric of the building – the Clean Bricks – which is where we will turn our attention to now.

3. The Clean Bricks

The Clean Bricks are made up of Clean questions – a specific set of questions asked in a structured way – which were developed in the 1980s by a counselling psychologist called David Grove.[2] He discovered that when he asked questions in this way he was able to minimise the risk of contaminating

2. Grove, D. and Panzer, B. (1989). Resolving Traumatic Memories: Metaphors and Symbols in Psychotherapy. New York: Irvington.

his clients' thinking with his own assumptions and interpretations, leaving them free to do their own thinking in their own way. This makes Clean questions the perfect tool for directing a person's attention to what emerges as they explore their current experience.

There is a set of 12 basic Clean questions (along with an additional 20 or so specialised questions). For the purpose of our exploration we will only use a selection of five of them, which I will be introducing to you at various stages throughout the book.

The rules to using Clean questions are simple and straight-forward:

- Listen carefully to what the other person says.
- Use only their word(s) along with a Clean question.

If you are asking Clean questions of yourself, then the same rules apply. Pay careful attention to the words you have used. Sometimes people choose to write their answers down or record them on their phone. Then take a word or phrase you have used and structure a Clean question around it.

We can get started straight away and have a go at using the Clean question that fits most easily into general conversation:

What kind of 'x'?
(where 'x' is a word or phrase that the person has just used)

Suppose someone says to us:

I've got some new ideas for this project.

We can create a number of different questions from the words that have been said:

What kind of new ideas for this project?
What kind of new ideas?
What kind of ideas?
What kind of project?

Notice how each question places our attention on different aspects of what has been said. Likely as not, whichever question we ask would generate some useful information.

Give it a go – jot down what you would say to someone who said:

She's driving me crazy!

For more information about Clean Language, visit: *www.thelisteningspace.co.uk/clean-language.*

Avoiding Misinterpretation
Being 'Clean' means that we simply accept what the person has said, without re-phrasing their words, and structure a Clean question around it. Wendy Sullivan and Judy Rees refer to this as 'parrot-phrasing' rather than paraphrasing![3]

---

3. Sullivan, W. and Rees, J. (2008). *Clean Language: Revealing Metaphors and Opening Minds*. Carmarthen: Crown House Publishing Ltd.

People's words are important to them, so honouring their choice of words helps them to feel acknowledged and respected. It also avoids misinterpretation. When someone uses a particular word or phrase it is easy to assume that we know exactly what they mean. The following activity demonstrates how different our interpretations of just one word can be.

We'll be adding in another commonly-used Clean question:

Whereabouts is 'x'?

ACTIVITY: Think of a Tree

Try this activity for yourself first.
You will be given a simple instruction, followed by a set of questions to answer.

Think of a tree.

What kind of tree is that tree?
Is there anything else about that tree?
Whereabouts is that tree?

This is the tree that you hold in your mind's eye at this moment in time. You could call this your ***mental model*** of a tree (unless, of course, you are looking at a real tree that exists in the space around you).

Now try this activity with 3 or 4 different people. Give them the same instruction, followed by the same set of questions.

You might want to invite each person to represent their tree on paper in some way – maybe using coloured pens or pencils, if you have them.

What did you notice?
- What differences did you notice between the different mental models of the trees that people have?
- Did the images help to highlight those differences?
- You may have noticed that I used a slightly longer version of the question, **What kind of** 'x'?

   What kind of 'x' is that/are those 'x'?

Asking the question in this way helps to make it sound a little softer.

The mental models we make will originate from our previous experiences – a tree we have seen in real life, for example, or in a film or book. When we compare the different mental models that people have of a tree, we notice that no two trees will be identical. There may be differences in (amongst other things):

- the type of tree – its colour, size or shape;
- the context that the tree is in – the season, the surrounding landscape;
- whether the tree is imagined or exists in reality;
- whether it looks real or like a drawing; and
- its location relative to the person in their mind's eye.

When one word alone can generate so many different models, it is easy to see how much scope for misinterpretation there is when it comes to a whole phrase or more complex concept, such as:

You need to show me more respect.
We need a strategic plan that accommodates the needs of our stakeholders.
Their work demands a very compassionate approach.

Within a split second we all of us create our own mental model of the words another person has used based on our own beliefs and assumptions, often without even realising it. So it's worth having a Clean question or two up our sleeve to check out how closely our interpretation matches the message the other person wants to get across. It enables us to do an internal 'press pause' and set aside the story that we are telling ourselves about what the other person has said.

Curbing Our Natural 'Righting Reflex'

Not only are these questions a great way of making sure that things don't get 'lost in translation' in general conversation, they also prevent us from acting on our natural desire to make things better (our 'righting reflex') when we are asking questions to help someone to explore what is on their mind.

I'll give you an example of what I mean by this. I recently asked a group of people how they might respond if someone said to them:

I'm stuck at a crossroads in my life.

Their most popular response:

Which path do you want to take?

On the face of things, this seems a very appropriate and helpful question to ask, but it assumes that:

- there are paths at this particular crossroads (and not roads);
- what needs to happen is to be moving away from this crossroads; and
- one of the paths is the way forwards.

We often ask questions that we think will guide a person to reach a solution to their problems. But who knows? In this instance perhaps what was needed was to stay put at the crossroads for a while or to take a metaphorical hot air balloon ride to get an aerial view of the situation. Asking Clean questions encourages the other person to explore their situation without contaminating their thinking with our assumptions:

What kind of crossroads?
Is there anything else about stuck?
Whereabouts are those crossroads?

As the other person gets a clearer understanding of their own situation in answer to these questions, any solution that appears is likely to be a best fit for their experience.

Ironically, when someone tries to help us, his or her well-intended efforts can end up having the opposite effect, leaving us feeling that we are somehow not capable. Perhaps there have been times when you've been offered a more 'balanced perspective' only to feel like your experience is being negated?

She was probably just trying her best.
I'm sure he didn't mean any harm by it.

People often describe being listened to 'Cleanly' as very liberating, and are surprised by their capacity to generate new, powerful insights and useful ideas that can make a big difference to their lives as a result.

Paying Careful Attention

Above all, asking Clean questions makes us listen like we've probably never listened before. Knowing that we will be repeating back another person's words means that we have to pay careful attention to the words that they use. In my experience, this often generates the kind of listening that Alice Duer Miller referred to when she wrote:

It means taking a vigorous, human interest in what is being told us. You can listen like a blank wall, or like a splendid auditorium where every sound comes back fuller and richer.

When we bring this quality of attention to our listening we encourage others to think and speak for themselves.

Practice Makes Perfect

For most people, using Clean questions takes a bit of getting used to – they may seem a little wooden at first. Some people find they can relax into this way of asking questions easily, whilst others find it takes a little longer. A little bit of practice is usually all that's needed. Just be patient and kind with yourself as you have a go. You'll find it easier to get your tongue round asking questions in this way with time, so don't give up if it seems somewhat unfamiliar at first.

Try experimenting with different types of intonation as you ask the question. You can make your voice sound puzzled, fascinated, intrigued or questioning, for example. In fact, the simple act of repeating back a person's words as if you are asking a question is often enough to encourage the person to explore their thinking further:

I felt so belittled and angry when she undermined me just then!

Belittled?
Angry?
Undermined you?

ACTIVITY: Clean Questions in Conversation

There will be numerous opportunities in the conversations that you have during the day when you can try asking the most conversational Clean question:

What kind of 'x'?
(where 'X' is a word or phrase that the other person has just used)

Next time you are in conversation with someone (a friend, colleague or family member, for example) try asking this question to find out a little bit more about what they have just said.

See if you can do this at least 10 times during the course of your day.

What did you notice?
- Did anyone start looking at you as though you were crazy?
- Perhaps you had to restrain yourself from giving your advice?
- What did you notice about the other person's response?

- Maybe you found yourself listening more, rather than thinking about what you were going to say next?

The interesting thing is that being asked these questions rarely sounds odd. I remember practising the questions with my own children:

I'm really hungry.
What kind of hungry?

I had a really annoying day today.
What kind of annoying?

I'm stuck with my homework.
What kind of stuck?

I noticed that richer conversations replaced otherwise monosyllabic responses. Before long, asking Clean questions became much more automatic and I found I was slipping them into other conversations. It gave the people I was talking with the opportunity to explain their situation before I jumped in with my own 'very helpful' suggestions. I became increasingly aware of just how many inaccurate assumptions I was making and how often my suggestions were not needed!

A Leap of Faith
You will soon find yourself using Clean questions in everyday conversations in order to avoid misunderstandings.

It can, however, take a leap of faith to use them to help

someone explore their thinking in the more in-depth way that we will be doing in this Lighthouse of Mindful Exploration. You will be invited to do activities that involve working with a fellow explorer at various stages throughout the book. As a facilitator you will need to trust that your explorer has the ability to find their own solutions to their situation; the less you do to try and help them, the more likely they are to gain insights and make changes that work for them. There may be times when they choose to talk about difficult thoughts and emotions, and you can never quite know where their exploration will lead them. At these moments you may need to sit with a degree of discomfort, confusion or uncertainty and resist the pull to go into 'fix-it' mode.

It is my belief that listening to others in this way is probably one of the greatest gifts we have to offer. Being listened to 'Cleanly' can be a profoundly liberating and empowering experience. It brings greater awareness of how we are living in our lives. In the words of someone who came across Clean questions at a parent workshop:

Clean questions can transform all aspects of your communication and understanding, at work, at school, and with family – no 'woo' or waffle – just a simple, profound method to bring clarity to your everyday talking and listening.

Summary

It's time to step in to the building, where we will be using Clean questions as a tool for mindful exploration.

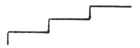

In the ground floor room that we are about to enter we will start by asking Clean questions of ourselves to help us tune in to our five senses, our thoughts and our emotions. You will then be invited to find a fellow explorer so that you can experience both asking and being asked these questions. As a facilitator (the person asking the questions) you will need to:

- set aside any desire to make things better;
- resist the urge to interpret and analyse;
- put to the back of your mind the clever thoughts and insights you feel the explorer ought to hear;
- slip into your back pocket all those experiences you want share so they know just how much you understand their situation;
- switch off your 'nosey brain'; and
- suppress any temptation to find out the juicy details.

Let's wipe our feet on the Welcome Mat and use the Key of Curiosity to open the door to wholehearted exploration.

Chapter 2

Being With Yourself

A bird does not sing because he has an answer.
He sings because he has a song.

Joan Walsh Anglund

As I explained in the introduction, my intention in writing this book is to show you how you can learn more about yourself in a creative way through metaphor and help others do likewise. By gaining self-awareness in this way, we see a situation with greater clarity. We may find that solutions which were previously hidden reveal themselves and we are able to take wiser and more considered action to change what needs to be changed.

Before learning more about metaphor in the next chapter, I'm going to invite you to spend time in this ground floor room, which is all about **Being With Yourself**.

Listening to yourself lies at the heart of all that we do in this book. We'll be doing plenty of activities that help you get in touch with your current experience. These activities are underpinned by the principles of mindful awareness, and you will gain benefit from doing them on their own, even if you do not go on to explore your experience through metaphor.

What is Mindful Awareness?

I remember when I was first introduced to the idea of mindfulness it all seemed rather mystical to me. When people talked about meditating I thought that this might be something that only those with some kind of special training and higher level of personal wisdom might be able to achieve, and that there was probably a right and a wrong way to being mindful.

But I've come to see mindful awareness as a very practical and down-to-earth process, based on a simple principle. It is about coming back to our senses – literally to what we are sensing in and around our bodies at any particular moment in time. For example, when I am washing my hands I might notice the sensation of water running over my skin, the texture of the soap on the palm of my hand and the movement of my hands, one over the other.

The mindset that we need to bring to this process involves:

- **non-judgemental observation** – so that we are able to acknowledge each aspect of our experience without judging ourselves or trying to change things. This means exploring our body senses, our thoughts and our emotions with a sense of open-minded curiosity;

- **an attitude of self-compassion** – so that we can be kind towards ourselves, particularly when we come face to face with more difficult emotions; and

- **acceptance** – so that we allow ourselves to be exactly as we are and this moment to be exactly as it is. This doesn't mean resigning ourselves to every disaster that comes our way or accepting the unacceptable. Rather, it means acknowledging our current reality and accepting our own responses to what is happening in each moment.

As Jon Kabat Zinn explains in his book, *Wherever You Go, There You Are*, mindfulness '*has to do with examining who we are, with questioning our view of the world and our place in it, and with cultivating some appreciation for the fullness of each moment we are alive. Most of all it has to do with being in touch.*'[4]

How Does Mindful Awareness Help Us?

By paying attention to our thoughts, feelings and emotions, we come to know ourselves better. We start to see each moment as it unfolds around us with more clarity. Rather than reacting to situations with all the worries and concerns from past events or imagined future happenings, we are able to respond to what is happening in a way that is more considered.

Whilst the process itself is subtle, the effects can be profound. Research shows that there are a number of ways in which

4. Kabat-Zinn, J. (1994). *Wherever You Go, There You Are: Mindfulness Meditation for Everyday Life.* London: Piatkus.

mindful awareness helps us deal with the pressures of everyday life:[5]

- Our stress levels decrease.
- We are better able to deal with symptoms of anxiety and depression.
- We are able to be more empathic and compassionate towards others.
- Our memory and concentration improves.
- Our immune system works more effectively.
- We become more creative.
- We sleep better.
- Our reaction times are faster.

We live in a world in which we are continually bombarded with information and advice. Mindful awareness helps us to connect with what feels right for us in the decisions we make.

It's easy to see why so many people are drawn to mindfulness. But we've got a bit of a paradox here. We are usually attracted to mindfulness for the benefits it can bring – who doesn't want to feel less stressed at times? Yet mindful awareness is about allowing ourselves to be exactly as we are and this moment to be exactly as it is. So, in order to realise any of the benefits, we have to let go of wanting them – a greater sense of wellbeing is just a side effect. This demands a trust in the process before you've even started, which requires another leap of faith!

5. www.evidence.nhs.uk/search?q=mindfulness

To help us make this leap, let's take a closer look at what we mean by coming to our senses.

Coming to Our Senses

As you stand and look about you in this warm and welcoming ground floor room of the **Lighthouse of Mindful Exploration**, you will see a set of seven big, brightly-coloured beanbag cushions scattered on the floor: each a different colour of the rainbow, each representing different aspects of our awareness.

The first five colours represent our five senses:

RED   What we are seeing.
ORANGE What we are hearing.
YELLOW What we are smelling.
GREEN   What we are tasting.
BLUE   Our bodily sensations.

You will be invited to sit a while on each of these five beanbags – not literally of course! We will be visiting each with an activity or two to help bring us to our senses.

We often lose touch with the way that our bodies feel as we grow to become adults. Increasingly we spend our time in autopilot, not being fully present in the current moment. We get caught up in our thoughts, reliving the past and planning an uncertain future. Our attention is often elsewhere.

But it wasn't always so for us. If you spend time with an infant or young child you become only too aware of how very connected we once were to our body senses and emotions:

- The desperate cry of hunger when it is time for a feed.
- The moments of total, undistracted immersion in play.
- The infectious belly laugh in response to a game of peek-a-boo.
- The angry scream when denied a favoured toy.

In fact, it can feel like a roller coaster of emotions at times! Our senses are never as raw and alive as they are at the early stages of our lives. As we grow older we learn to modify and suppress our bodily responses and manage our discomfort and distress. But we also lose much of the intensity of joy and excitement that we once felt as a child. Increasingly we end up 'living in our heads'. In our busy, task-oriented lives we get distracted and caught up in our thoughts at the cost of registering what is happening in and around our bodies.

Think back to when you first got up this morning. What were you sensing from the moment you awoke? Did you notice the feel of the floor beneath your feet? Or the particular tonal quality of the sky as you opened the curtains? What sounds of life did you hear from the world outside? Did you savour each mouthful of food as you ate your breakfast? Or perhaps, like me, you were distracted by the day's to-do list. It was only when I reminded myself to pause and look out of the window that I noticed just how breathtakingly beautiful the colours of the sunrise were.

When we are in touch with our senses we find new ways of waking up to the world. Time seems to slow down as we savour the richness of each unfolding moment. We experience afresh the things that we may have been taking for granted:

- The transient beauty of a sunset.
- The feel of the ground beneath our feet.
- The joyful sound of birds singing.
- The heady scent of flowers in a summer's garden.
- The subtle mix of flavours in a mouthful of food.

Connecting With Our Thoughts and Emotions

The final two coloured beanbag cushions represent our thoughts and emotions:

INDIGO   Our thoughts.
VIOLET   Our emotions.

The activities at these two cushions will be about noticing the continual stream of thoughts and associated emotions that arise for us. When we pay attention to our thoughts we notice how they come and go, rather like bubbles floating past on the surface of a stream. Instead of getting caught up in the flow, we can choose to step onto the bank and watch our thoughts as they pass by. We see them for what they are: transient mental events. One thought follows another. And another. And another. Sometimes getting swept furiously along in a torrent of floodwater, sometimes drifting gently on by.

All the time, we are giving meaning to our experiences. We sort back through the filing system of our mind and see situations through the filter of who or what they remind us of. Remember the metaphoric helmet with its **Visor of Certainty** that was mentioned in the last chapter, filtering the things we see and hear to fit with our mental model of how the world works? Unwittingly, we become trapped in our own interpretation of events and our emotions reflect this. We believe the reality as we see it to be the only reality.

When we are in touch with ourselves we start to separate out the information we receive from our senses from the meaning that we are making of it. We come to appreciate that our thoughts don't have to control us and that we have a choice about whether or not to act on them. It becomes easier to catch negative thoughts before they slip into a downward spiral.

For those of us who have an irresistible urge to take difficult situations personally this can come as a bit of a revelation! Even if only for a moment, we can put down the stick of shame that we love to beat ourselves up with and simply listen to what our inner critic has to say on the matter – and most inner critics have a lot to contribute! Rather than judge our thoughts, we can choose to observe them with compassion and say to ourselves:

This is how it is for me in this moment.

Removing the Armour

Being in touch means removing our metaphoric helmet with its **Visor of Certainty** so that we see and hear what is happening around us with greater clarity and separate this from our interpretation of events. It also means removing our **Flak Jacket of Perfection** that keeps us pretending to be the person we feel we ought to be rather than allowing ourselves to be the person that we really are. It means putting down our **Shield of Safety** that we use as a barrier to engaging with others to protect ourselves from rejection and loss.

When we remove this armour we allow ourselves to be just as we are and each moment to be just as it is. Many people describe a sense of coming home to themselves, of coming to know themselves better, and a sense of gaining control of their lives.

Setting a commitment to being in touch with ourselves will underpin all that we do in this chapter and indeed throughout our tour of this Lighthouse of Mindful Exploration. But this is not something we can just talk about or absorb from the pages of a book. This is a practical process. We have to set the intention to pay attention – and then get on and do it!

Before We Begin

Most of the activities are short meditations lasting no longer than ten minutes. You will need a timer for these activities so you can keep the focus of your attention on the meditation itself rather than needing to watch the clock.

It is not intended that the meditations be done one straight after another, although there is nothing to stop you doing so should you choose to. Rather, you might want to return to a beanbag cushion and repeat that particular meditation a few times over the course of the following days. Or you could take a 'pick and mix' approach to the colours that you visit over the course of the week – red and yellow one day, green the next day, indigo and orange the day after. Even if you already have a regular meditation practice, you might want to enjoy spending time with the activities that follow.

Getting Warmed Up

We're going to start with a warm-up activity that's about bringing more focus to the things we do as we go about our daily lives. Most of us have to make a conscious decision to do one thing at a time, especially in a technology-driven world which demands that our attention is pulled continually in so many different directions:

- We answer the phone whilst having a drink with friends.
- We respond to texts whilst watching a movie.
- Increasingly we see our life through the lens of the camera on our mobile phone – unless of course we are too busy using our phone for some other purpose instead!

Much of the time we find ourselves multi-tasking whilst keeping half an eye on an ever-growing to-do list – rushing from one activity to the next in an attempt to be more productive, more efficient. But inevitably there comes a point where we end up achieving less as our stress levels rise and we are less able to concentrate. The sense of continually 'chasing your tail' takes its toll on our sense of wellbeing.

However, when we focus on one thing at a time instead of having a myriad of tasks on the go at once, time appears to slow down. It's as if we somehow create time. We also start to see the world in a richer, more vibrant, and more textured way.

So let us now begin…

ACTIVITY: One Thing at a Time

Set your timer to 10 minutes.

There's no need to take time out of your day to do this activity. You can carry on with whatever activity you had planned. As you do so, silently name to yourself each thing that you do.

Here's an example taken from the running commentary that went on in my head when I did this activity earlier this morning:

Now I'm sitting down at my computer.
Now I'm reading an email.
Now I'm making a note in my diary.

Simply acknowledge each action in turn. That's all there is to it! Have a go.

What did you notice?
- Did you find yourself slowing down a little to take notice of what you were doing in each moment? or
- Were you frustrated and wanting to rush one thing to get on with the next?

- Don't worry if you found it difficult to keep your attention on the task in hand. The fact that you noticed that this was happening for you is mindful awareness in action!

Try repeating the activity in small, bite-sized chunks during the day, each time adding a little more detail.

ACTIVITY: Adding Detail

Each time you practise *One Thing at a Time*, see if you can add a little more detail, more texture to the running commentary in your head. Rather than just listing the things you are doing, start to **describe the things that you are noticing** as you go along.

For example, you might notice the things that you are seeing or hearing, or the sensations in your body:

I'm noticing the cool feel of the glass against my hand.

I'm noticing the sound of birdsong as I walk along this footpath.

I'm noticing the tension in my right shoulder as I sit at my computer.

I'm noticing the deep red textures of the rose in the vase.

Awareness is the key. Recognising what is happening in our bodies is the first step to shifting what's happening in our mind. Imagine, for example, that you are feeling stressed – your mouth is dry, your muscles tense, your heart racing. It might seem counterintuitive to pay attention to these unpleasant body sensations, but being able to observe these symptoms without judgement means we are less likely to get caught up in any associated negative emotions. We can say to ourselves:

This is my experience in this moment.

Now that we're warmed up to paying attention to what is happening in each moment, let's visit those Rainbow Cushions.

The Rainbow Cushions
We will be doing a short meditation at each cushion. I'm going to call these **Clean Meditations** because they will involve using the Clean questions that were introduced in the previous chapter to bring our focus to the different aspects of our awareness:

What kind of 'x'?
Is there anything else about 'x'?
Whereabouts is 'x'?
(where 'x' is a particular aspect of our experience)

At the start and finish of each meditation we'll spend a few minutes bringing our attention to notice our breath as it flows in and out of our body. The breath is like an anchor in mindful practice, a way of drawing our attention back to our senses when our mind has wandered. It is a constant – we bring it with us everywhere we go!

If you're new to meditation, don't worry – there is nothing magical or mysterious about what we're about to do. You are not aiming to clear your mind, but rather notice what is on your mind as you bring your attention to any particular aspect of your experience.

Every time you notice your mind has wandered, simply bring your attention back to the aspect on which you are focussing. And take it from me, your mind will wander! There are times when my mind seems to be in continual motion – rather like the fluttering of a butterfly, randomly changing direction, only coming to settle briefly before it takes off again.

Although it can be very frustrating when your mind keeps flitting from one thought to the next, remember that this is normal. Noticing that your mind has wandered is in itself being mindful and you can congratulate yourself for setting aside the time to be with your experience.

For each of the meditations that follow, there are free recordings to download from *www.thelisteningspace.co.uk/recording-meditations*. However, you can simply follow the written instructions if you prefer. You might find it helpful to close your eyes after each question as you bring your attention to that particular aspect of your experience.

ACTIVITY: Tuning in to Your Breathing

Set your timer to 3 minutes.
Settle yourself into a comfortable position – you may choose to be sitting, lying or standing.

Bring the focus of your attention to your breathing:

Whereabouts do you notice your breathing?
What kind of breathing is that breathing?
Is there anything else about that breathing?

After each question simply pause (for 10 seconds or more) to notice where your attention goes.
If your mind wanders at any point, as it will, bring it back gently and with kindness to the focus of the question.

Continue to notice your breathing:

Whereabouts do you notice your breathing *now*?

What kind of breathing is that breathing?
Is there anything else about that breathing?

Gently open your awareness out to your surroundings as you near the end of this meditation.

 Go to *www.thelisteningspace.co.uk/recording-meditations* for a free download of a recording of this meditation.

What did you notice?
- Did you become easily distracted?
- Did you notice any changes in your breathing?

You will be tuning in to your breathing at the start and finish of every meditation from now on, so it is worth practising this breathing meditation several times before we move on to visit the Rainbow Cushions. With practice you will find that these three Clean questions become increasingly familiar and easily remembered:

Whereabouts do you notice your breathing?
What kind of breathing is that breathing?
Is there anything else about that breathing?

It's now time to visit the first of our beanbag cushions.

The RED Beanbag: SEEING

This red beanbag cushion is all about bringing the focus of our attention to the things that we see around us. The following meditation will give you the opportunity to really take notice of the things that you are seeing.

ACTIVITY: Seeing

Set your timer to 5 minutes.
Settle yourself into a comfortable position – you may choose to be sitting or standing.

Before you begin, take a few minutes to tune in to your breathing.

Start your timer and gradually soften your gaze as you open your awareness to the things you see around you. Rather than naming the objects that you see or thinking of their function, simply notice:

- the shapes and contours that you see;

- the colours and shades;
- the way the light catches different objects; and
- the spaces between the things that you see.

When the timer stops, bring your attention back to your breathing for a minute or two.

 Go to *www.thelisteningspace.co.uk/recording-meditations* for a free download of a recording of this meditation.

What did you notice?
- It's not unusual to have the kind of experience that one person described to me:

  It was like seeing things for the first time – really vivid, very defined and clear. It really sharpened my focus. Initially things felt detached from me, and then gradually I started seeing things in relation to me.

The ORANGE Beanbag: HEARING

Let's move to the orange beanbag cushion to focus our attention on our hearing. We tend to pay more attention to the things that we see around us and take less notice of the things that we hear. This next meditation is about tuning in to those sounds that you hear.

ACTIVITY: Hearing

Set your timer to 5 minutes.
This meditation can be done whilst out for a walk or you may choose to be sitting, lying or standing instead.

Before you begin, take a few minutes to tune in to your breathing.

Start your timer and gradually open your awareness to the sounds that you hear around you. Close your eyes if that makes it easier for you. Rather than thinking about what might be causing these sounds or how you feel about them, simply be curious about the qualities of the sounds that you hear. What do you notice about their:

- tonal qualities – are they high or low pitched?
- volume – are they loud or soft?
- resonance – do you sense their vibration in your body?
- rhythm – do they have a particular rhythm, like the call of a bird or hum of an engine?

Ask yourself the following Clean questions:

What kind of sounds are those sounds?
Is there anything else about those sounds?
Whereabouts are those sounds?

After each question, pause to notice where your attention goes. If your mind wanders at any point, just bring it back gently and with kindness to the focus of the question.

When the timer stops, bring your attention back to your breathing for a minute or two.

 Go to *www.thelisteningspace.co.uk/recording-meditations* for a free download of a recording of this meditation.

What did you notice?
• Were there sounds that you were previously unaware of?

The YELLOW Beanbag: SMELLING

Time to tune in to our sense of smell. Some of us are more sensitive to smells than others, so don't worry if you find that there aren't any strongly-defined smells available to you during this meditation.

ACTIVITY: Smelling

Set your timer to 5 minutes.
My suggestion is that you do this meditation whilst out walking – perhaps while taking a stroll round the garden or the next time you are out on an errand.

Before you begin, take a few minutes to tune in to your breathing.

Start your timer and bring the focus of your attention to the smells that might be available to you. Simply be curious about the qualities of each smell that you notice and ask yourself the following Clean questions:

What kind of smell is that smell?
Is there anything else about that smell?
Whereabouts is that smell?

Pause to notice where your attention goes after each question. You may want to get closer to the things that have a scent – a particular flower, for example.

If your mind wanders at any point, just bring it back gently and with kindness to the focus of the question.

When the timer stops, bring your attention back to your breathing for a minute or two.

Try repeating this activity at a time when there are different scents around you – while eating a meal perhaps.

 Go to *www.thelisteningspace.co.uk/recording-meditations* for a free download of a recording of this meditation.

What did you notice?
• Did you find that there were smells available to you?

Many of us pay little conscious attention to our sense of smell (unless of course you're a wine taster or chef) and yet smells can be powerfully evocative. Have you ever found yourself transported back to a vivid holiday memory by a particular smell? The smell of garlic, for example, that brought you back to a holiday in the Mediterranean.

The GREEN Beanbag: TASTING

Let's tickle those taste buds with a bit of mindful eating on this green beanbag cushion.

ACTIVITY: Tasting

This meditation is often done with a single raisin, but it can be done with anything that you choose to eat.

Before you begin, take a few minutes to tune in to your breathing.

Then take one small bite of the food and pause. Hold that small mouthful on your tongue before you chew. Notice the tastes that are available to you and ask yourself these Clean questions:

What kind of tastes are those tastes? (*sweet, sour, salty, or bitter*)
Is there anything else about those tastes?
Whereabouts are those tastes?

After each question, pause and become really curious about your experience.

Now slowly and deliberately start to chew that small mouthful of food. Again, notice the tastes that are available to you and ask yourself the above three Clean questions.

When you have finished that one mouthful, pause to

bring your attention back to your breathing for a minute or so.

You may then want to repeat the activity with another mouthful of food.

 Go to *www.thelisteningspace.co.uk/recording-meditations* for a free download of a recording of this meditation.

What did you notice?
- Were there any flavours that surprised you?

The BLUE Beanbag: BODILY SENSATIONS

Move on round to the blue beanbag cushion for the next meditation. It's time to tune in to our bodily sensations. Just as there may be sights, sounds, smells and tastes which are available to us that we are not consciously aware of, there may also be sensations in our bodies that we only notice when we pay conscious attention to our body. For example, take a moment to notice any tension that you may be experiencing in your body, or the feeling of your hand touching this book.

ACTIVITY: Bodily Sensations

Set your timer to 5 minutes.
Settle yourself into a comfortable position.

Before you begin, take a few minutes to tune in to your breathing.

Start your timer and bring the focus of your attention to the sensations in your body. Take a slow and deliberate scan of your body, starting from your head and going all the way down to the tips of your fingers and to the tips of your toes.

Notice any bodily sensations that you have.
Simply be curious about the qualities of these sensations. Choose a sensation that you would like to explore and ask yourself these Clean questions about it:

What kind of sensation is that sensation?
Is there anything else about that sensation?
Whereabouts is that sensation?
Does that sensation **have a size or shape**?

When the timer stops, bring your attention back to your breathing for a further minute or two.

 Go to *www.thelisteningspace.co.uk/recording-meditations* for a free download of a recording of this meditation.

What did you notice?
- Were there any bodily sensations that you were previously unaware of?

You may have noticed that I've sneakily introduced a new Clean question:

Does 'x' **have a size or a shape**?

Some people are surprised to find that there is an almost physical form to the bodily sensation that they are exploring. Here are some examples from recent explorations:

A pain in the neck that feels like a thick, coiled rope causing the explorer to tense their shoulders.

A pressure inside the head that feels like the walls in the movie, 'Labyrinth', closing in around them.

A calm, relaxed feeling like a will-o'-the-wisp ball of energy between the lungs.

A pulled muscle at the top of the hip like a rough-edged

rock from the beach that catches as they move.

Tension all around the top half of the body like a big iron armour on the outside crushing inwards.

The question **Does 'x' have a size or a shape**? invites the explorer to notice whether the sensation they are exploring has a tangible form in this way.

In this Lighthouse of Mindful Exploration we will only ever be using five of the total 30 or so questions that exist in the full Clean Language repertoire. But I'm afraid you'll have to wait until Chapter 4 before you meet the remaining question.

The INDIGO Beanbag: THOUGHTS

Having focussed our attention on the different senses in our body, it is now time to tune in to our thoughts on the indigo beanbag cushion. In this meditation you will be invited to become an observer of your thoughts – to notice them come and go with a detached curiosity. Simply acknowledge your thoughts, without judging them. It can help to silently name them as they appear:

I'm worrying about what he will think about me.

I'm excited about developing this project.
I'm thinking that people won't want to support me.

It's not uncommon to find that you judge yourself in relation to practising these mindful activities:

ACTIVITY: Thoughts

Set your timer to 5 minutes.
Settle yourself into a comfortable position.

Before you begin, take a few minutes to tune in to your breathing.

Start your timer and bring the focus of your attention to your thoughts as they come and go. You might want to silently name the thoughts that you are having.

Just be curious about these thoughts and ask yourself these Clean questions:

What kind of thoughts are those thoughts?
(planning for the day ahead, mulling over past events, gratitude for the people in your life)
Is there anything else about those thoughts?

When the timer stops, bring your attention back to your breathing for a minute or two.

 Go to *www.thelisteningspace.co.uk/recording-meditations* for a free download of a recording of this meditation.

What did you notice?
- Were you able to name the kind of thoughts as they arose?

The Drama Triangle

At this point, I'm going to introduce you to the Drama Triangle, which is a way of unpicking your thoughts. Because of its beautiful simplicity, many people find this model a very useful way of naming the kind of thinking that they are doing when things aren't working so well for them – when they are 'in drama'. Stephen Karpman suggested that in these situations we tend to adopt one or more of the following drama roles: **Persecutor**, **Victim**, and/or **Rescuer**.[6] Since our thoughts drive our behaviours, having a greater awareness of our thinking helps us to understand why we might be reacting to a situation in a particular way. Let me introduce you to each of these roles in turn:

The Persecutor believes that someone else or something else is at fault. They blame others, make them feel guilty and point out that they are wrong and need to change. This tends

---

6. Stephen Karpman created the Drama Triangle as a social model for understanding the destructive and changing roles people play in conflicts.

to lead to conditions of competitive one-upmanship.

The Victim believes that either they aren't good enough or the situation they are in is hopeless. They believe they are powerless and are quick to point out that nothing can be done.

And to complete the drama triangle...

The Rescuer believes that others can't manage without them and they need help in some way. They train victims to become more disempowered and placate persecutors whilst building up stored anger towards them.

Rescuing Versus Helping

There are many situations, both in our personal and our professional lives, where helping others is an important part of what we do.

I see a distinction between helping and rescuing.

Helping is a 'choice-full' act – both on behalf of the person helping and the person being helped. The person being helped is empowered to make decisions about the kind of help they would like to receive. The person offering help is able to say '*I choose to*', rather than '*I have to*'.

Being 'in Drama'

The following page shows the kind of things that we might find ourselves saying (inwardly or out loud) when we are 'in drama'. Do any of these phrases sound familiar to you?

The Drama Triangle

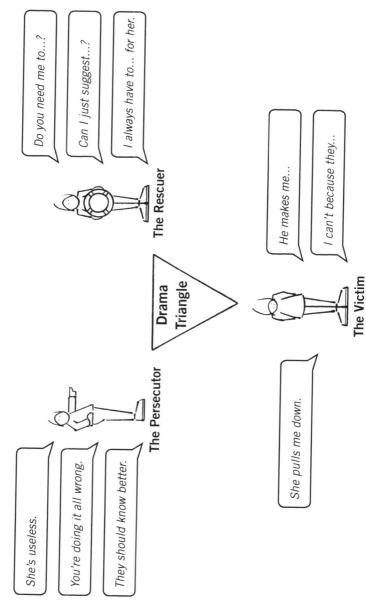

Do you need me to...?

Can I just suggest...?

I always have to... for her.

The Rescuer

He makes me...

I can't because they...

The Victim

She's useless.

You're doing it all wrong.

They should know better.

The Persecutor

Drama Triangle

She pulls me down.

Perhaps you have found yourself playing one or more of these roles at work or in your personal life? Personally, I'm a bit of an expert Rescuer! But I'm also an accomplished Persecutor and Victim. In fact, you can even become Persecutor of yourself (you can *give yourself a hard time*).

We don't necessarily play the same role every time and it is quite possible to play two or more roles in the same scenario. Let me give you an example. A friend told me that his mother recently made this comment to him: '*I just want you to be successful.*' There was something about this seemingly supportive comment that made him feel uncomfortable and when he unpicked his thoughts he noticed an element of each of the drama roles in his thinking:

Victim: *She thinks I'm not successful and that makes me feel inadequate.*

Persecutor: *Why can't she accept me for who I am? She's so judgemental.*

Rescuer: *If I put everything into making this project a success then I can make her happy.*

We all enter into drama from time to time – it is part of being human and is impossible to avoid entirely. There is no one role that is better or worse than the other. The key is to notice when we are in drama, to own and accept our responses and to realise that we can choose not to act on them.

Now that we've spent time tuning in to our thoughts, it's time to visit the final beanbag.

The VIOLET Beanbag: EMOTIONS

This violet beanbag is all about tuning in to our emotions. We're going to start with a fun activity to challenge our emotional vocabulary, because one of the things that helps us become more aware of our emotions is an ability to name them as we experience them.

ACTIVITY: An Alphabet of Emotions

Take each letter of the alphabet in turn and see how many emotions you can find for each. I'll get you started with a couple of emotions for A-E:

A   apprehensive, anxious
B   bored, blue
C   curious, confident
D   devastated, daring
E   excited, ecstatic

See if you can add to the list I've created and complete the alphabet – but don't worry, I'll let you off X!

There are some examples at the end of the chapter – I'm sure you'll be able to think of more.

We're going to make our emotions the focus for this next meditation.

ACTIVITY: Emotions

Set your timer to five minutes.
Settle yourself into a comfortable position.

Before you begin, take a few minutes to tune in to your breathing.

Start your timer and gradually bring your awareness to your emotions.

What emotion are you drawn to exploring?

What kind of emotion is that emotion?
Is there anything else about that emotion?
Whereabouts do you feel that emotion?
Does that emotion **have a size or a shape**?

At the end of the five minutes bring your attention back to your breathing for a minute or so.

Go to *www.thelisteningspace.co.uk/recording-meditations* for a free download of a recording of this meditation.

What did you notice?
- Were you able to identify any particular emotion?
- If so, could you find a location for it?

Again, people are often surprised to find that there is an almost physical form to their emotion. Here are some examples that I've come across recently:

An anxious feeling like a knot of rope coiled up in the stomach.

A feeling of confusion like dark tangled fibres in the head.

A feeling of overwhelm like a wave crashing over the head.

A feeling of joy like a bright yellow light glowing from the chest.

A teacher who felt love towards the children in her class like the warm, red glow of the 'Ready Brek' child – for those of you who are old enough to remember the advert!

So we've now spent some time at each of the Rainbow Cushions, tuning in to the different aspects of our awareness. We're going to complete this chapter with an activity that explores our experience by bringing together different elements of our awareness – through the evidence from our senses, our thoughts, and our emotions. At this point I'm going to invite you to find a fellow explorer to work with because you will probably find more benefit from doing this activity with a partner and taking it in turns to ask the questions of one another.

Mapping Your Experience

The following activity helps to separate the information from our senses, in particular what we are seeing and/or hearing, from the meaning that we are making of a situation or event. It is adapted from the Clean Feedback Model.[7]

If you choose to do the activity with a partner, you will need to make sure that:

- anything that is said will be held in confidence; and
- the explorer has plenty of time to consider their answers – the whole activity can take up to 20 minutes each way.

Alternatively, you can do this activity on your own and ask the questions of yourself. Either way, make sure that you read the full set of instructions before you begin. You might also find it helpful to read the example on p78-80 before doing the activity.

---

7. Doyle, N. and Walker, C. Cleaning Up the 'F' Word in Coaching www.cleanlanguage.co.uk/articles/articles/272/1/Cleaning-up-the-F-word/Page1.html7

ACTIVITY: Mapping Your Experience

You will need four pieces of paper or post-it notes. Label them as follows:

Evidence	**Thoughts**	**Emotions**	**Drama**

Lay your pieces of paper out in a line on the floor as shown above.

The explorer will stand on each piece of paper in turn – guided by the facilitator, who will ask the questions in the order given below.

You may want to write the answers on a separate piece of paper.

Starting question:
Is there a situation that happened recently that you would like to explore?

What were you seeing?
What were you hearing?

What story were you telling yourself about the situation?
What were you assuming about yourself?

Emotions

How were you feeling in this situation?

If you are exploring a situation that didn't work so well for you:

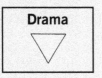

Drama

Did any of the drama roles resonate for you in relation to this situation?

Victim?
   If so, is there anything else about being Victim?
Persecutor?
   If so, is there anything else about being Persecutor?
Rescuer?
   If so, is there anything else about being Rescuer?

You can encourage the explorer to expand on each of their answers by asking:

Is there anything else about 'x'?
(where 'x' is a word or phrase that they have just used)

To invite some final reflection ask:

Was the story you were telling yourself true?
Is there a different story available to you?

What did you notice?
- Were there any surprises for you as you explored your situation in this way?
- Was there a different story available to you?

EXAMPLE: in this example, the person was exploring a situation involving his manager that hadn't worked so well for him.

Evidence:	*My manager didn't give me any feedback after a presentation that had taken me three days to prepare.*
Thoughts:	*She didn't think it was any good.*
	She doesn't value my efforts.
	I'm not as capable as my peers.
Emotions:	*I feel inadequate and unimportant.*
	I was annoyed and upset after going to so much effort.

Drama:

Persecutor:	*My manager doesn't value her staff and isn't very good at recognising all the work that I do.*
Victim:	*Nobody realises how hard I've worked.*
	They don't recognise my abilities.
Rescuer:	*I would have said something but I don't want her to feel awkward.*

Notice just how much meaning was ascribed to this one event – all the thoughts and emotions that were generated for this person. His assumptions may well have been correct, but it's also possible that there were other ways of viewing the situation, as he realised with the reflecting questions:

Was the story you were telling yourself true?
I know that I'm capable really.
I've had good feedback for other presentations that I've given.

Is there a different story available to you?
Maybe she's distracted by something.

She may have thought the presentation was excellent. Unless he asks her he may never know.

People are often surprised by just how much they are making up about a situation when they physically separate things out in this way. However, allowing ourselves to be the irrational, imperfect and inadequate beings that we are is often a necessary step to being ready to restore a sense of balance and perspective.

Each time you practise this activity it becomes easier to do this separation. Soon you'll notice yourself starting to pause and take a step back to challenge the assumptions that you are making about a situation rather than jumping to conclusions and reacting from a position of drama.

Summary

This chapter has been about **Being With Yourself**. We have used various activities that are underpinned by the principles of mindfulness, along with Clean questions, to tune in to the different aspects of our awareness: our five senses, our thoughts and our emotions.

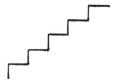

It's now time to climb the stairs to the first floor, **The Room of Metaphor**, where we will take a look at how uncovering the metaphors that we use naturally can bring rich insights about ourselves and the situations we find ourselves in, and reveal solutions to our problems that are a best fit for us.

Suggested answers to AN ALPHABET OF EMOTIONS
(p73)

A	apprehensive, anxious
B	bored, blue
C	curious, confident
D	devastated, daring
E	excited, ecstatic
F	furious, frustrated
G	glad, generous
H	happy, hopeful
I	impatient, irritated
J	joyful, jealous
K	kind, knowledgeable
L	loving, lonely
M	magnificent, morose
N	nervous, numb
O	optimistic, overwhelmed
P	pessimistic, proud
Q	quizzical, queasy
R	rested, resentful
S	sad, serious
T	troubled, traumatised
U	unsure, unsafe
V	vexed, vulnerable
W	worried, wishful
Y	youthful, young-at-heart
Z	zealous

Chapter 3

The Metaphor Room

The ability to simplify means to eliminate the unnecessary
so that the necessary may speak.

Hans Hofmann

Welcome to **The Metaphor Room**!

In the last chapter, **Being With Yourself**, we spent time exploring our current experience by paying attention to our various senses and to our thoughts and emotions. Rather than letting our thoughts control us, we came to see them as 'mental events' that come and go, like clouds passing in the sky.

In this chapter, *The Metaphor Room*, we will be introduced to another means of exploring our current experience, by uncovering the metaphors that underpin our thinking. In the introduction I mentioned that metaphor means describing one thing in terms of another. Remember the friend who described a feeling of tension like big armour crushing inwards on the top half of her body? We are often unaware of these metaphors, but Clean questions can be used to encourage them to emerge from the words that we use. These metaphors are unique and give us powerful, revealing insights into the way that we are experiencing the world.

But before we go any further, let's shine the spotlight of attention on metaphor itself.

How Is Metaphor Important?

It is not difficult to describe things that are tangible and have a form, like an object or an animal. There will be words we can use to represent the physical qualities of the thing we are describing. The laptop that I am writing on, for example, is silver with black keys. It also has a location – on top of my desk. When we are describing a thing that is real and has tangible form we can use information that relates to our five senses: what we see, hear, smell, taste, and our bodily sensations.

But when it comes to describing abstract concepts, like confidence or courage, there is no physical thing to see or hold. Instead, we often have to rely on using a metaphor. For me, confidence means being strong and rooted, like a tall horse chestnut tree. This metaphor captures the essence of my inner experience. For someone else, confidence might have quite different qualities – perhaps being powerful and free, like an eagle soaring high in the sky. These metaphors are unique to each of us. Even if, by strange coincidence, your confidence is also a tall horse chestnut tree, it won't be in the same location with exactly the same qualities as mine.

Metaphors pack a lot of information into a memorable 'bundle' – painting a more detailed picture than the words we use to describe our experience. They reflect our **mental model** of a situation – the way we are thinking about our experience.

In their book, *Metaphors we Live By*, Lakoff and Johnson wrote:

> *In all aspects of life … we define our reality in terms of metaphors and then proceed to act on the basis of these metaphors. We draw inferences, set goals, make commitments, and execute plans, all on the basis of how we in part structure our experience, consciously and unconsciously, by means of metaphor.*[8]

Since our metaphors are a reflection of the way we structure our thinking, which in turn determines our behaviours, a change in metaphor will often result in a change in the actions we take. There is a fascinating account of a coaching session by a Clean Language facilitator called James Lawley, which illustrates this beautifully.[9] His client talked about wanting to '*be able to hold the line against aggressive senior managers.*' Here are some of the metaphors he used to describe his situation:

> *I blew up.*
> *I was in a Catch 22 situation.*
> *His method is to drill you and then attack.*
> *The troops are falling by the wayside.*
> *I can lose it in the heat of battle.*

---

8. Lakoff, G. and Johnson, M. (1980). *Metaphors We Live By.* Chicago: The University of Chicago Press.
9. Lawley, J. (2001). *Metaphors of Organisation – Part 2.* www.cleanlanguage.co.uk/articles/articles/20/

When James repeated his words back to him, he replied that he was 'shell shocked' and needed to 'defend his territory' to be on 'the winning side'. No guesses as to his underlying metaphor for work: a battle! This was the metaphor on which he was basing his thinking and his actions. Once he was made aware of this he was able to identify that there were choices available to him. He decided that he no longer wanted to live by this battle metaphor. Instead he chose the metaphor of an orchestra:

He used the (new) metaphor to gauge his and others' behaviour: Am I participating like a member of an orchestra? When am I the first violinist and when am I playing the triangle? When I chair a meeting, are we all playing the same tune and am I conducting appropriately?

The manager recognised that seeing his work as a battle had significantly influenced the way he responded to his colleagues, and in particular those 'higher up the command chain'. Over the next few months he gradually altered his behaviour to more closely fit his orchestra metaphor. And surprise, surprise, senior managers started acting differently towards him.

As James put it, he'd gone from using 'bombs to batons' in his relationship with senior colleagues.

We have much to learn from our own metaphors:

- They condense a great deal of abstract information into a tangible and memorable package. This is particularly useful when it comes to describing more complex concepts that are emotionally charged or difficult to define, such as respect or compassion.

- They get to the heart of the matter quickly, enabling us to think in deeper, more profound ways.

- The metaphors we choose represent a physical structure that mirrors the experience they symbolise in real life. These structures may be resourceful and empowering, but they may also be self-destructive and disempowering. Having an awareness of our metaphors often reveals choices available to us which were previously hidden.

- When we link two ideas that don't usually belong together through metaphor, we often come to understand things in new ways. Einstein's Theory of Relativity, for example, resulted from his imagining what it might be like to travel on a beam of light.

- Metaphors have form, and since they have form they can change: a key can unlock a door, a bird can fly the nest, a torch can light the way. These changes occur naturally and spontaneously, given the opportunity to do so.

The following activity created by Penny Tompkins and James Lawley brings home just how important metaphor is to the way we experience the world. Take a moment to complete this activity before reading on.[10]

ACTIVITY: A Handful of Coins

Find a handful of coins and place them in the palm of your hand. Notice their size, shape, weight and colour. What does this set of coins mean to you?

- The cost of your next drink at the café?
- The price of a daily newspaper?
- Money for the parking meter?

Choose coins from this set to represent you and each of your family members or closest friends. Arrange them on the surface in front of you.

Take a moment to reflect on how you chose the particular coin to represent each person symbolically. Was there any significance in the attributes of the coins?

- The size?
- The shape?
- The colour?
- The way that you arranged the coins in relation to one another (their spatial arrangement)?

10. Sullivan, W. and Rees, J. (2008). *Clean Language: Revealing Metaphors and Opening Minds*. Carmarthen: Crown House Publishing Ltd.

Now imagine that, for reasons beyond your control, one of them has to be removed. Which one do you choose to remove?

What did you notice?
- You probably had no difficulty in understanding how to use the coins as a metaphor for each of the people you chose because we are 'hardwired' to think in metaphor.
- Most people find that giving the coins metaphoric representation means that when they are asked to take one away they have an emotional response. This is because they have attributed emotional significance to the coins they have chosen.

Metaphor gets to the very essence of things. It often generates an experience that is richer emotionally than using abstract conceptual language alone. But perhaps the thing that I like most about metaphor is that it opens the door to a person's thinking in a way that is so utterly intriguing and compelling. Ask questions of a person's metaphor and before you know it you have a story unfolding in front of your eyes. So often I've heard people respond to discovering their own metaphors by saying, '*These metaphors are magical!*'

In fact, other people's metaphors can be so appealing that you end up being influenced by them yourself. A fellow Clean Language facilitator and author of *Clean Language in the*

Classroom,[11] Julie McCracken, once shared with me her metaphor for holding boundaries kindly and firmly in the classroom:

> *I'm soft and furry like the Honey Monster (only pink). Friendly, warm and comforting … with a brick wall inside … firm … solid.*

The next time I found myself in the middle of one of my daughter's toddler tantrums I paused and thought to myself, *What would I need to be like to be that Honey Monster with a brick wall inside?* It was like clicking on a computer hyperlink to a state of calm and loving firmness: a shortcut to a much more resourceful way of managing the situation.

Metaphor is particularly suited to mindful exploration because it gives form to:

- the big issues of life – the things that give us a sense of meaning and purpose, such as being able to make a difference to the lives of others;
- ill-defined feelings – when something feels wrong, unsafe or missing;
- issues of identity and spirituality – who am I in the various roles in my life?;
- internal conflicts – our struggles with getting a good work-life balance, for example; and
- the patterns of thinking and acting that don't serve us, or are destructive to us – such as always putting the needs of others ahead of ourselves.

11. McCracken, J. (2016). *Clean Language in the Classroom.* Carmarthen: Crown House Publishing Ltd.

Interestingly, exploring our experience through metaphor also seems to create an inherent sense of safety. Rather than talking about the details of the experience itself, we talk about our situation in terms of something else, making more sensitive issues seem less threatening to explore.

A Partial Picture

It is, however, important to be aware that whilst metaphor sheds light on some aspects of an experience, it can leave other aspects in the dark. Gareth Morgan explains how metaphors persuade us to understand situations in a partial way.[12] They create insight but they also distort our thinking. He illustrates this with an example – the way we talk about organisations as a machine. When an organisation works well it *'runs like clockwork'*, like a *'well-oiled engine'*. When it is not working well we need to *'get to the nuts and bolts of it'*, to *'fix it'*, and intervene at the *'point of maximum leverage'*. Employees are *'cogs in a wheel'*, the *'manpower'* that is managed by human *'resource'* departments. This mechanical view leaves no room for organic development and cross-fertilisation of ideas.

Since metaphors influence the meaning we attach to the original experience and the decisions and actions we take as a response, it is in our interest to pay attention to the metaphors that we use. Metaphors can be a source of creativity but they can also be a self-imposed prison that keeps us stuck in patterns that don't serve us. Gaining awareness of the structure of our thinking through metaphor often reveals choices that can have a profoundly transforming effect on the life that we lead. We may decide, for example,

12. Morgan, G. (1986). *Images of Organization*. Beverley Hills: Sage Publications.

to exchange bombs for batons!

The Surprising Way in Which Metaphors Shape Our World

Metaphor is at the very heart of the way we think. There have been some fascinating developments in the field of cognitive linguistics over the past 30 years that have furthered our understanding of the way in which metaphors shape our world.

The metaphors we use are derived from our understanding of the body and the physical world around us. So when we describe a person as being cold, we aren't usually referring to their body temperature! We are using concrete qualities to describe an abstract concept: affection is warmth. You could say that metaphors have their 'roots' in the physical world – which, of course, is a metaphor in itself! From the moment we are born, as we learn about each new thing, we think about it in terms of what we know already. Our brains are programmed to spot patterns and make connections with previous experiences. We build up a bank of comparisons, a network of personal metaphors that reflect our life's learning so far. This is how we develop our understanding of the way that the world works. We would otherwise have to learn everything afresh, as if for the first time, from the moment we get up each morning.

If we take the origin of the metaphor above, **affection is warmth**, as a small child explores their world they learn that love and affection means, amongst other things, being kept warm physically. From this a whole host of metaphors are generated:

She had a warm smile.
The temperature of the meeting dropped.
She's a bit of a cold fish.
A hotline to my heart.
They greeted us warmly.

To take another example: **important is big**. The child soon realises that important things, like the adults around them, are big in terms of both size and weight. And so we get more metaphors:

It's a weighty issue.
Today is your big day.
It was a great opportunity for him.
I was being belittled.
High priority.

There have been some fascinating studies that explore the relationship between metaphors and their physical roots – their link to our experience of the world as we grow and develop. A number of studies have taken a concept along with its physical representations and noted what happens if you change either side of the metaphoric-physical equation.

Affection is physical warmth: people were asked to read a description of an individual and rate their personality.[13] Those who were given a cup of hot coffee to hold beforehand were more likely to rate the personality of the individual as warm, compared with those who were given a cup of iced coffee.

---

13. Williams, L. E., and Bargh, J. A. (2008). *Experiencing Physical Warmth Promotes Interpersonal Warmth. Science.* 322 no. 5901 pp. 606-607.

Physical warmth influenced the rating of metaphorical warmth.

The effect was shown to work in the opposite direction too.[14] People who were asked to recall a time when they felt ostracised, or 'left out in the cold' socially, gave lower estimates of room temperature than those who recalled an experience where they were included socially. Metaphorical warmth influenced the rating of physical warmth.

Here are another couple of examples of concepts that have been explored.[15]

Rigidity and strictness is physical hardness: people who sat on soft, cushioned chairs were more willing to compromise in price negotiations than those who sat on hard chairs.

Importance is physical heaviness: people who were given a CV for a job applicant on a heavy clipboard were more likely to rate the applicant as taking their job more seriously than those who were given a light clipboard.

These findings highlight an interesting aspect of the way in which our brains process information from the world around us. The idea that our thinking is linked to our bodies in this way is known as embodied cognition. It appears that the same parts of the brain process both the literal and metaphoric versions of a concept – the parts of the brain we call the insula and anterior cingulate. Our brains are less bothered

---

14. Zhong, C.B., and Leonardelli, G.J. (2008). *Cold and lonely: does Social exclusion literally feel cold?* Psychological Science. 19, 838-42.
15. Ackerman, J., Nocera, C., and Bargh, J. (2010). Incidental Haptic Sensations Influence Social Judgments and Decisions. Science Jun 25: 328 (5986): 1712-1715.

about the symbolic and the real than we might suppose and we really are hardwired to think in metaphor.

You'll probably start noticing metaphors everywhere you look after reading this chapter! Metaphors are clearly fundamental to the way we think, make decisions and experience the world. Gaining access to them can give us valuable insights.

This is where the **Clean Bricks** of this **Lighthouse of Mindful Exploration** play such a vital role. By asking Clean questions of the metaphors that we naturally use, we help to bring them out from the shadows into the light of day. However, many metaphors are quite subtle and hidden from view and we first need to be able to spot them as they arise. So this is where we will turn our attention to next: developing our metaphor-spotting skills.

Metaphors, Metaphors Everywhere!

There is a beautiful scene in Michael Radford's Italian film, *Il Postino*, which gently sums up the way in which metaphors appear all around us. The film revolves around the relationship between Mario Ruoppolo, a fictional character, and the exiled Chilean poet, Pablo Neruda. Mario is a simple postman, who is very much in awe of Neruda and keen to learn more about his poetry and politics. In this particular scene the two are sitting together in conversation, looking out to sea. Neruda creates some lines of poetry that describe the sea. In response to hearing his words, Mario inadvertently hits upon his own metaphor:

Mario: *I felt like a boat tossing around on those words.*

Neruda:	Like a boat tossing around on my words? Do you know what you've just done, Mario – you've invented a metaphor.
Mario:	No!
Neruda:	Yes, you really have.
Mario:	But it doesn't count because I didn't mean to.
Neruda:	Meaning to isn't important – images arise spontaneously.
Mario:	You mean that, for example … the whole world with the sea, the sky, with the rain, the cloud … the whole world is a metaphor for something else?

Exactly so, Mario. The whole world is a metaphor for something else. And metaphors do just arise spontaneously.

You might want to have fun coming up with some metaphors of your own with the activity on the following page inspired by Marian Way.[16]

16. Way, M. (2013). Clean Approaches for Coaches: How to Create the Conditions for Change Using Clean Language and Symbolic Modelling. Portchester: Clean Publishing.

ACTIVITY: Metaphoric Body Scan

In the previous chapter we took a physical body scan of the sensations in our bodies. This time I'm going to invite you to do a metaphoric body scan and see how many metaphors you can think of that relate to the different parts of your body.

I'll get you started with a few:

- Out of your mind.
- Head and shoulders above the rest.
- Take a good nose around.
- Pay lip service.
- Try your hand.
- Get your foot in the door.

Your turn now:

Take a scan from top to toe. How many metaphors can you find?
You could pool resources with a friend and see if you can come up with an even more comprehensive list.

There are more suggestions at the end of the chapter.

These are just some of the metaphors that I have come across in the course of my day so far that involve the five senses:

Sight	*The apple logo on my iPod.*
	The wedding ring on my finger that symbolises my marriage.
	The thumbs up gesture that a friend gave me.
Sound	*The church bells that mark the passing of time.*
	The siren of the ambulance signifying an emergency.
	The love song on the radio.
Smell	*The smell of roast dinner that symbolises family time together.*
Taste	*The taste of coffee symbolising connection with a friend.*
Bodily sensations	*The gut feeling I have about the man who fixed my bike.*

Whenever we associate one experience with another, we have the makings of a metaphor. Here's an activity that explores the associations that you make when you think of a person that you admire.

ACTIVITY: Who Do You Admire?

Think of a person that you really admire.
This person can be alive or dead, famous, a friend or family member – or simply an acquaintance.
Choose up to 6 words you would use to describe why you admire this person:

-

-

-

-

-

-

Take a moment to reflect on the words that you have chosen.

Are these qualities that you hold important in other areas of your life?
- Your personal life?
- Your social life?
- Your work life?

People often find that the qualities they admire in the person they have chosen reflect values that are important to them in their life in general. You could say that the person they admire is in some ways a metaphoric representation of their core values.

The metaphors that we naturally use tell us a lot about the way we are experiencing the world. The more that we become attuned to these metaphors, the more we can learn about ourselves from them.

Probably the easiest metaphors to access are in the words that we use. So this is where we'll start in developing our metaphor-spotting skills.

Developing Your 'Metaphoric Ears'

What kind of ears are 'metaphoric ears'? Ears that pick up the metaphors in the words that you hear people use as they speak.

Suppose someone says to you:

> *I'm standing at a crossroads,*
> or
> *He put me down.*

Whilst these statements may literally be true, it is more likely that they are being used to describe a situation in terms of something else, which makes them metaphoric. The clue is in the context. If the person in the first example is talking about facing significant life decisions, then the statement is more likely to be metaphoric than a reference to their position at a road junction! Ask yourself: *Is this person describing something that is literally happening?* If the answer is no, then the statement is metaphoric. Is the person in the second statement talking about a person that made them feel inadequate or was he literally being lowered down?

Sometimes the clue to metaphor is more obvious. We know that one situation is being described by another if the statement starts with one of the following phrases:

It is like …
It's as though …
It reminds me of …
It's similar to …

Technically speaking these statements are similes – a figure of speech in which two unlike things are compared – rather than metaphors. However, for the purpose of exploring the metaphors that people naturally use as an expression of their inner experience, we treat both simile and metaphor alike. And from this point onwards in the book I shall refer to both as metaphor.

On the following page there is an activity to practice your metaphor-spotting skills in the language people use.

ACTIVITY: Taking It Literally

One way of deciding whether a statement is a potential metaphor is to determine whether or not you can **do the action**. If you have a statement describing an action but you cannot physically do the action, then you have a metaphor.

Here are some examples for you to work through. Decide whether you can **do** the following statements in real life:

- Open the door.
- Open up opportunities.
- Push the boundaries.
- Push his buttons.
- Take it out on me.
- Take it out of the box.
- Think outside the box.
- Put him down.
- Put him on the spot.
- Eat your words.
- Eat your dinner.

What did you notice?
- Did you find yourself thinking that some statements were possible to put into action, but could also be used to describe something else? We would need to know the context before deciding whether the statement was literal or metaphoric.

When we start to pay attention to the metaphors in people's words, we notice them everywhere: in conversations, on the radio or television, in newspapers, books and magazines. Perhaps it is not surprising that studies suggest that there are as many as six metaphors a minute in the language we use,[17] maybe even more – it's just that we aren't usually aware of them.

Take, for example, an interview I heard on an episode of the Radio 4 programme, *In the Moment*. The interviewee was talking about his experience of playing 'improv jazz' (the metaphors are in bold):

> *A bit like **sailing**, you know like **catching the wind**. That feeling like where you've **put the sail up** that doesn't mean that **the wind goes in the sail**. You've got to **find wind**. You've got to **find that gust**, and if you **get in it** you can **keep it going**.*

The metaphors in this interview were obvious with all its references to sailing. But many metaphors are more hidden. Here are some that have already appeared in this chapter:

Cultivating mindful awareness
Uncovering metaphors
Developments **in the field of** cognitive linguistics
Examples for you to **work through**
On the radio

17. Pollio, H.R., Barlow, J.M., Fine, H.J., and Pollio, M.R. (1977). *Psychology and the Poetics of Growth: Figurative Language in Psychology, Psychotherapy and Education.* Hillside, NJ: Lawrence.

Here's an activity that will help you to further develop your 'metaphoric ears'.

ACTIVITY: Tuning in to Metaphor

Turn on the radio or television and listen carefully to the words. Don't worry about following the meaning of what is being said, just tune into the words. See if you can spot any metaphors – both those that are more obvious and those that are more hidden.

Remember, there are **clues to help you decide whether something is metaphoric**:

- The statement starts with the phrase 'it's like', 'it's as if', or 'it's as though'.
- What is being talked about is not literally happening.

See how many metaphors you can find as you tune your attention in to the words that you hear.

Try listening to a recorded interview. You might find that you catch more metaphors each time you listen in.

What did you notice?
- Could you spot any metaphors?
- With practice your 'metaphoric ears' will become increasingly sensitive and you'll start to hear metaphors everywhere!

However, as we've already seen, metaphor isn't limited to the words people use. The coins activity earlier in the chapter showed us just how readily we ascribe symbolic significance to the objects we see around us. Here are some other examples of using one thing to represent another:

- **Gestures:** a thumbs up, a wave, a shrug of the shoulders.
- **Non-verbal sounds:** a sigh, gasp, 'hmm' or 'ahh'.
- **Posture and body language:** a foot tapping, a gaze or facial expression.
- **Creative expression:** through music, dance and art.
- **The stories** that we tell.
- **Our rituals and traditions:** a wedding ceremony, giving of flowers.
- **Objects:** advertising, religious icons.
- **The uniforms** we wear.

Since many of the metaphors we use are visual, we also need to develop our 'metaphoric eyes', which is where we'll turn our attention to next.

Developing Your 'Metaphoric Eyes'

And what kind of eyes are 'metaphoric eyes'? Eyes that notice the potential metaphors in the things we see around us: in a gesture, a movement or piece of art.

The following activity will get you focussing your 'metaphoric eyes'. You could also do this activity with a partner, taking it in turns to be facilitator and explorer. Make sure you read the instructions before starting the activity. There are two completed examples on p108-10. You may want to read these before doing the activity yourself.

ACTIVITY: Choose an Object

Read the following instructions before you try the activity yourself. You will need a pen and paper on which to record your answers.
The activity usually takes 10-15 minutes to complete. If you are doing the activity with a partner, give them plenty of time to form their answers. They will appreciate not being rushed.

Choose a concept or issue to explore. Some examples that others chose when they first did this activity include:

- self-confidence;
- my wellbeing;
- my creativity; and
- my relationship with my partner.

Write your chosen concept or issue down: if the issue is a complex one, find a word or short phrase that would summarise what you want to explore.

Pause and take a minute to tune in to your breathing: close your eyes if you wish. Give yourself time to bring your attention to yourself in this present moment. Then, when you are ready, bring your awareness back to the room around you.

Look all around you: notice the things that you see.

Choose an object that represents the concept or issue you have chosen in some way.

Then answer the following questions:
What drew you to the [object]?

Is there anything else about what drew you to the [object]?
Is there anything else about what drew you to the [object]?
Is there anything else about what drew you to the [object]?
Is there anything else about what drew you to the [object]?

And what do you know now about all of that?
And what difference does knowing this make?

There is space for writing your answers on p111-2.

Bear with the repetitive nature of the questions. As someone recently said to me, '*I thought "not again!" But each time you asked me if there was anything else it made me dig deeper and think more about my choice.*'

When you are asking the questions of someone else, try bringing different intonation to the way that you ask each of the repeated questions. This will help you sound curious and inviting.

If your explorer answers '*no*' before you have asked them all the repeated questions, then just move on to the final two questions, which invite them to reflect on what they have discovered. But bear in mind that, given a little space, people will often find further thoughts come even after answering '*no*'.

And finally, it isn't even necessary for you to know what the explorer's chosen issue is. They can simply let you know what their object is. This can help the explorer to feel a greater degree of safety if the issue they have chosen is a particularly sensitive one.

EXAMPLE 1: in this example, someone else asked the explorer the questions.

Topic of exploration: *My relationship with my partner.*
Object chosen: *The big plant.*

What drew you to the big plant?
It's not uniform. It's got shape and it's actually got a bit that's growing out all on its own.
It's random, solid and quite tall.

Is there anything else about what drew you to the big plant?
It's got some structure but it's also not uniform.
There's something about it just being different in that way.

Is there anything else about what drew you to the big plant?

It's varied; each leaf is individual but it's on the main stem.
But I really like the fact that it's got a whole new shoot, and I hadn't noticed this until now.

Is there anything else about what drew you to the big plant?
It's quite a big shoot, that's suddenly gone off – it seems to be separate.

Is there anything else about what drew you to the big plant?
It feels quite hopeful actually. How lovely is this!
And it's going towards the window.

And what do you know now about all of that?
It's quite resilient. And it's grown a long way.

And what difference does knowing this make?
How lovely is that!

EXAMPLE 2: in this example the explorer did the activity on his own, writing his answers on a piece of paper.

Topic of exploration: *Working with his illness rather than fighting it.*
Object chosen: *The picture of a chimp on the wall.*

What drew you to the picture?
He can be playful – I can use humour to engage with

him. If he bares his teeth, I need to come beside him and soothe him, not face him head on.

Is there anything else about what drew you to the picture?
He's part of nature. He is a precious part of this world.

Is there anything else about what drew you to the picture?
He exists as part of a system, of which we are all equally important with our own needs and feelings.

Is there anything else about what drew you to the picture?
He needs love and compassion – an open heart and support.

Is there anything else about what drew you to the picture?
We need to keep perspective on what's important, on the grand scheme of things.

And what do you know now about all of that?
To keep bringing love and humour to the situation – to be alongside him and wait for him to be ready. Connection and support is what really matters.

And what difference does knowing that make?
It makes me feel a lot calmer and more accepting – more resourceful.

Your turn now. Write your answers on the following pages.

Answers to CHOOSE AN OBJECT

Topic of exploration:

Object chosen:

What drew you to the [*object*]?

Is there anything else about what drew you to the [*object*]?

Is there anything else about what drew you to the [*object*]?

Is there anything else about what drew you to the [*object*]?

Is there anything else about what drew you to the [*object*]?

And what do you know now about all of that?

And what difference does knowing this make?

What did you notice?
- What did you notice as you chose the object?
- What did you notice as you answered the questions?

Some people have enjoyed this activity so much that they have chosen to use it as a kind of daily meditation. It helps them pause to really take notice and connect with what is important to them.

Here's another activity to exercise your 'metaphoric eyes'.

ACTIVITY: Take a Walk

Time for a fresh air break!
Choose a walk that you would like to take. It could be a walk around town, in a local park, or out in the countryside – anywhere that you are drawn to walking.

You might find it helpful to bring a notebook and pen to

jot down the answers to the following questions as you go, or record your answers on your phone.

Before you set off, choose a current situation that you would like to explore.

Once you are established in your walk, pause for a moment to look around you.

Ask yourself the following questions:
How does what I see around me inform me about my current situation?

Is there anything else about what I'm noticing?
Is there anything else about what I'm noticing?
Is there anything else about what I'm noticing?
Is there anything else about what I'm noticing?

And what do I know now about all of that?
And what difference does knowing that make?

What did you notice?
- Did you find that there was symbolic significance in the things that you saw around you?

It is also useful to train our 'metaphoric eyes' to notice the gestures that people use. These gestures often hold symbolic meaning, even though the person may not be consciously aware of making them.

ACTIVITY: Spot the Gesture

If you watch carefully, you will notice that often people answer questions with their body by making gestures before any words come out of their mouth. Here are a couple of examples that I have come across recently:

- A mother cradling her hands over her heart when talking about her teenage daughter.
- A friend gesturing with a horizontal hand at forehead level as she explained, '*I've had it up to here with the situation.*'

It is well worth developing your ability to spot gestures because of the significance they may hold.

See what gestures you notice next time you:

- have a conversation with a friend;
- watch a programme on television; or
- look around you as you sit in a cafe.

What did you notice?
- Perhaps there are some gestures that seemed to be more significant than others?
- If so, how did you decide that this was the case?

A Word of Caution

At this point I'm going to add a word of caution. It can be very tempting to analyse other people's metaphors, visual or otherwise. Remember that we are in a *Clean* Lighthouse of Mindful Exploration. We are acting as observers of what is. It is not our role to read the mind of others – in fact, I'm quite sure that this would not be possible even if we wanted to. We can never really know what is significant for another person. There have been times, for example, when I have been very wrong in assuming that a person was not feeling emotional about the experience they were talking about just because of the lack of gesture or expression in their tone of voice.

If you find yourself wanting to make judgements, just as I had done, then remind yourself of the **Welcome Mat** that you wiped your feet on before entering the building. When you wipe away any desire to analyse, fix, change or judge, you leave space to simply acknowledge and accept the metaphors that arise for people, yourself included.

Summary

Now that we've warmed up our 'metaphoric ears and eyes', we're ready to move on up to the next floor, ***Being With Others***.

On this floor you will be invited to work with a practice partner so that you can learn how to create a Listening Space for one another, using Clean questions to invite exploration in a way that encourages metaphors to reveal themselves.

But before we do that, I'm going to share with you another story of Clean exploration through metaphor that I particularly love. Tompkins, Sullivan and Lawley wrote about a school counsellor working with a child who was becoming '*emotionally disturbed from an inability to learn maths*.'[18] The boy explained that when he tried to do mental maths it was like '*tangled spaghetti*' in his head. He was asked some Clean questions to find out more about this spaghetti:

What kind of tangled up?
Is there anything else about that spaghetti?
Whereabouts in your head is that tangled spaghetti?

After answering, he paused for thought and said:

It wants to have water poured on it so it can slip free and then dry in the sun.

Some more Clean questions. Suddenly the boy exclaimed:

Oh look, the spaghetti has squashed together into one piece. It looks like a piece of paper and I can put my numbers on it.

Now that the he had a place to see the numbers in his mind's

---

18. Tompkins, P., Sullivan, W., and Lawley, J. (2005). Tangled spaghetti in My Head: Making Use of Metaphor. Available at http://www.cleanlanguage.co.uk/articles/articles/30/

eye, he could learn maths – a solution that only he could have discovered for himself and a beautiful example of the magic of metaphor in action.

- Splitting hairs
- A head start
- Brainwashed
- At the back of my mind
- Face up to something
- Eyeball it
- Turn the other cheek
- Have a nose around
- Pay lip service
- On the tip of my tongue
- Chin up
- Shoulder the burden
- Put some elbow grease into it
- Keep someone at arm's length
- Give someone a hand
- Tight-fisted
- Wrap them round your little finger
- Heart warming
- Navel gazing
- Talking out of your backside
- Getting a leg up
- Putting your best foot forward

Chapter 4

Being With Others

Out beyond ideas of wrongdoing and rightdoing,
there is a field. I'll meet you there.

When the soul lies down in that grass,
the world is too full to talk about.

Ideas, language, even the phrase 'each other'
doesn't make any sense.

Rumi

Welcome to the second floor of this **Lighthouse of Mindful Exploration.** In this room we will be combining the elements we have already encountered on our tour of the building to create a space of exploration for others – a **Listening Space**. But before we do so, let's just remind ourselves of the story so far.

On *Entering the Building*, we wiped our feet on the **Welcome Mat**, removing any desire to fix, change, or judge ourselves or others. This is an essential step to creating the conditions for accepting the whole range of thoughts and emotions that might arise for us.

We used the **Key of Curiosity** to open the door to a mindset of open-minded enquiry. This building invites us to become curious about how things 'actually' are rather than judging ourselves or others when things aren't the way we feel they 'ought' to be.

We removed the metaphoric armour we wear to protect ourselves from vulnerability:

- We hung up the **Flak Jacket of Perfection** that keeps us pretending to be the person we feel we 'should' be in order to fend off criticism.
- We put down the **Shield of Safety** that we hold up as a barrier to engaging with others in an attempt to avoid failure, rejection and loss.
- We removed our helmet with its **Visor of Certainty** that convinces us that we have the 'right' way of seeing things.

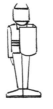

We took notice of the **Clean Bricks** from which the lighthouse is constructed. These bricks are formed from Clean questions – a specific set of questions asked in a structured way. We saw how these questions can be used to invite a person to expand on what they have just said without contaminating the interaction with our own assumptions and interpretations, whether this is in general conversation or in more in-depth exploration.

The ground floor room was all about *Being With Yourself*.

Here we spent time tuning in to the various aspects of our experience by visiting each of the seven brightly coloured **Rainbow Beanbag Cushions** – representing our five senses, our thoughts and our emotions.

We learnt how to separate out, or unpick, the whole host of thoughts and emotions that arise for us from what is actually happening, and noticed just how much meaning we give to things that may not be the reality.

In order to gain further insights into the type of thinking that we are doing we were introduced to the **drama roles** that we tend to adopt when situations aren't going the way we would like them to.

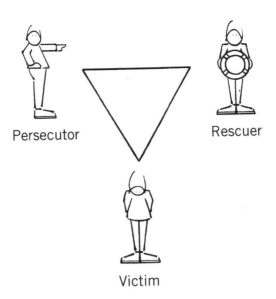

Persecutor

Rescuer

Victim

The focus of attention on the lower floors of the building has been on ourselves. This is because we first need to have awareness of our own thoughts and emotions in order to be able to listen well to others. There may be times when the person we are listening to says things that trigger uncomfortable feelings for us and we find ourselves 'in drama'.

We may feel the pull to become **Rescuer**, with a desire to make things better:

Have you thought about …?

Or notice impatience in our inner **Persecutor**:

Come on, the solution is obvious!

Or catch our inner **Victim** having a moan:

It's always me who has to do the helping!

At such times we will need to sit with our discomfort as we give the explorer the freedom to do their own thinking. It can be helpful to simply acknowledge our experience inwardly, with compassion, and remind ourselves that it is not our role in this lighthouse to fix or judge.

Moving up to the first floor, ***The Room of Metaphor***, we saw how metaphor (describing one thing in terms of another) captures the essence of our experience in a way that is more tangible and memorable. Exploring the metaphors that we naturally use to describe our experience can be a very powerful way of coming to know ourselves better.

A friend once described this beautifully:

Metaphor creates the starting point for a story. When a metaphor comes to your mind you can ask yourself: How will I use this to move forward in my story?

This brings us up to the second floor, which is about ***Being With Others***. In this chapter you will be taken step by step through the process of creating a Listening Space for others, bringing together the various components that we have encountered so far in our journey up the building: using Clean questions to bring awareness to our experience, often through metaphor.

You will be encouraged to work with a partner so that you can put these steps into practice. This will give you a chance to be both facilitator and explorer. Meaningful practice is dependent on the explorer bringing issues that are real for them rather than imagined scenarios, as happens in role play activities.

It will take practice for the whole process to become familiar, so go easy on yourself while you are learning. Before long, you will find things become easier.

What Is a Listening Space?

A Listening Space is a process in which one person facilitates another to explore an issue that is on their mind, using a combination of repeating back their words and a specific set of Clean questions. This can be done with friends, relatives, colleagues or clients – so long as there is an element of trust between you and the other person would value having the space to explore their thinking. Their exploration could be about anything from a problem they would like to gain clarity on to a creative idea they want to develop.

As I explained in the Introduction, a Listening Space can be used by anyone and should not be confused with counselling, coaching, or therapy – although professionals who work with others in this capacity may find this process a very useful addition to their toolkit.

Before you begin your listening, you will both need to wipe your feet on the metaphoric **Welcome Mat** and set aside any desire to fix things. This is a space where all thoughts and emotions are welcome, in equal measure. It is not a space for asking clever questions or rushing in to make things better. Instead we work on the assumption that people make useful choices when they are encouraged to gain awareness of themselves and do their own thinking. This makes Clean questions the perfect tool for the job, since they help us put our assumptions and suggestions to one side.

By shining a **Clean Light of Attention** on the person doing the exploring in this way, you will be creating the conditions that encourage powerful new insights to be generated, creative ideas to form, and solutions to difficulties to reveal themselves. People will often surprise you with the quality of their thinking when they can relax in the knowledge that they won't be judged, analysed or interrogated. When we resist the temptation to fix and make better, and trust a person to find their own solutions to the challenges they face, we often find ourselves in the privileged position of being a witness to some truly inspiring thinking.

When I'm facilitating this process, I imagine that the explorer is like a goat (yes, a goat!) tethered to a post. The post represents the focus of their exploration. They are free to graze as far as they like in any direction. With each question, I bring their attention back to the tethering post to encourage more in-depth discovery.

As a facilitator of a Listening Space, your intention is neither to understand your explorer nor to share their feelings. Rather, you are creating the conditions for them to figure themselves out. This process is about encouraging the explorer to create a relationship with the things that they are discovering about themselves, rather than creating a relationship with you. It is almost as though you become invisible as they put all their attention on their own experience.

At first it can seem a little unfamiliar, uncomfortable even, to hand over responsibility so fully to the other person. But this session is for their benefit and is not about having things explained for your understanding. You are prevented from asking 'nosey' questions to satisfy your own curiosity. There will likely be times that you have to sit with a certain degree of confusion about what is being said. If you are prepared for this, then it is less likely to faze you.

Be patient and open to the possibility of change happening spontaneously as the explorer gains fresh insights. In fact, ironically, the less you try to help, the more things are likely to change of their own accord. Since the explorer is free to decide which direction they take in their exploration, any ideas or solutions they arrive at are likely to be a best fit for them.

THE SIX STEPS TO CREATING A LISTENING SPACE

There are six easy-to-follow steps to creating a Listening Space:

Step 1: Starting the session.
Step 2: Establishing the tethering post.
Step 3: Exploring the tethering post.
Step 4: Creating an image.
Step 5: Exploring the image.
Step 6: Ending the session.

I'm going to take you through each of these steps in turn. But before I do so, I'll explain how to set the scene for holding a Listening Space. I'll also be sharing some handy hints for being a facilitator.

SETTING THE SCENE

There are some important aspects to setting the scene for holding a Listening Space for someone.

Creating a Safe Environment

Creating a safe environment for exploration is crucial, particularly where vulnerable thoughts and emotions are concerned, or if you are likely to come across one another in a social or work context.

The following rules of engagement help to ensure that conditions of safety are established and maintained:

1. There needs to be **mutual agreement** that creating a Listening Space is what is wanted in the first place.

2. **Confidentiality** must be respected. What is said in the Listening Space stays in the Listening Space, unless the content of the session is raised at a later date by the explorer or they give you their permission to share their words.

3. To make sure that both of you can be fully present in the process, set aside some **uninterrupted time** for your Listening Space.

Having a clearly defined time frame also helps to prevent you going 'into drama' with your explorer. You might otherwise find your inner voice saying things like:

Rescuer: *If I just give them some more time they'll have a chance to figure this out.*

Victim: *Oh no! I've got so much I could be getting on with and they've still got more to say.*

Persecutor: *OK, enough now. You're going on and on and the solution is so obvious!*

Initiating a Listening Space

You can initiate a Listening Space in one of two ways:

1. You agree to create a Listening Space for its own sake.
2. One person brings an issue up in general conversation and the other asks them something like:

Would you like to explore that in a Listening Space?

Since a Listening Space is not a normal kind of conversation, you will first need to get the other person's explicit agreement. I usually explain what is involved by saying something like this:

I'd start by asking: *What would you like to explore?*

I'd then be repeating back your words and asking a specific set of questions.

This space would be about exploring what's on your mind, rather than having to come up with solutions.

Whatever you say in the Listening Space stays in the Listening Space, unless you tell me that you would like it to be otherwise.

There might be times when you don't want to answer

out loud. If so, then you can sit with your thoughts for as long as you need before letting me know that you are ready for another question.

I would probably write some of your words down to help me remember what you've said. You could take a copy at the end as your own reminder.

Is this something you would like to do?

If the person says 'yes', then agree on a mutually convenient time for some uninterrupted listening. The process usually takes about 20 minutes and can be done in person, over the telephone or over some form of internet video conferencing (via Zoom, for example). You do not have to be able to see one another to be able to listen with careful attention. Some people actually prefer to be listened to when they are not sitting face-to-face with their listener.

Using a Listening Space Within a Professional Listening Session

I find The Listening Space an invaluable tool to use within the coaching work that I do. Since I already have a contract to work with the client, it is not necessary to give an explanation of the process beforehand. Instead, if the client uses a word or short phrase that seems important to them or emotionally charged, I might say:

Is this something you would like to explore in more depth?

If the answer is 'yes', then we use this as the tethering post and see what insights may be gained – rather like having an island of Listening Space within the session. Sometimes there are several islands of discovery to be had. And there may be times when the exploration is so fertile and in-depth that the Listening Space takes up the whole hour-long session.

THE LISTENING SPACE PROCESS

Once you have mutual agreement and have set aside some uninterrupted time together, you are ready to hold a Listening Space for the other person. I'm going to outline what's involved in this six-step process. These instructions are followed by a transcript taken from a recent Listening Space session that gives an idea of what can happen when people are asked Clean questions in this way.

I would recommend that you read the whole chapter before you try holding a Listening Space for someone else.

Step 1: STARTING THE SESSION

Start the session by asking:

What would you like to explore?

With this question you are opening the gate to the imaginary field of your explorer's mind. You are inviting them to graze around any thoughts and emotions they have at that moment. Just sit back and be curious. Give your explorer your undivided attention as you listen to what they have to say. They will often start with a general rambling. A bit of grazing here. A bit of grazing there. This is all part of the exploration. Trust that they can figure things out given time.

Sometimes you will notice the explorer pause from his or her grazing – chewing the cud if you like. If you see that they are still deep in thought, wait patiently and hold the silence around them. Even though you may find it uncomfortable to do so, they will be grateful that you haven't rushed them. This is the kind of silence that seems to be alive with their thinking. They may still have more to say.

Sooner or later your explorer will look to you for their next question.

This may be after a single word:

Facilitator: What would you like to explore?
Explorer: *Frustration.*

It may be after a few sentences:

Facilitator: What would you like to explore?
Explorer: *A feeling that I sometimes get when I feel my blood pressure is going up. Whether it's due to things that are going on at work, or the children, or anything else. I get that feeling of, not impending rage, but it just feels like things are getting to the overload stage. It feels like pressure inside my head.*

Or it may be after a whole belly-full of grazing!

Facilitator: What would you like to explore?
Explorer: *The fear of rejection has been another component of what I want to connect to. I want to explore the notion of the fear of rejection, and then I might be able to see some connections to that. There certainly seems to me to be a limiting factor in what I do that I often don't go for things I should do because I have a sudden kind of panic. I definitely have a notion that the two are connected. The fear of rejection is like a skin of oil that restricts and constricts me; the more I try to free myself, the tighter it gets. It gets stronger as I try to fight it sometimes. It constricts me.*

It covers me.
Increasingly it's not there.
Sometimes I'm really trapped by it.
Sometimes I'm not.
So, I guess I'm not really sure what the two
states are. Why should it be sometimes my
fear gets initiated, sometimes it doesn't? It's
not consistent.

Listen carefully to what your explorer says. In the next two stages of the process you will be repeating some of the words they have used.

Step 2: ESTABLISHING THE TETHERING POST

When your explorer looks up after their initial grazing, you will be inviting them to make a decision. Explain to them that:

- You are going to repeat back some of their words.
- You would like them to let you know which word or short phrase resonates most for them.
- This will then become the focus for their exploration.

This focus word or short phrase will be the post to which you tether them. They will be free to graze as far as they like in any direction. Each time they look up from their grazing you will be bringing them back to the tethering post with your questions – rather than letting them graze randomly throughout the field of their mind.

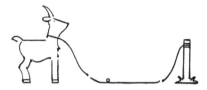

The only choice you need to make at this stage is which words to repeat back as potential focus words. You cannot be wrong in your choice, so long as they are words that the explorer has used.

However, there are words that seem to prompt more fruitful exploration – namely, the **embodied** words that the explorer has used.

What do I mean by embodied? These are words that describe something that is happening in or around that person's body. The most obvious example being a word that describes a **feeling**, such as:

Joy	*Desire*
Anger	*Excitement*
Love	*Envy*

But in a Listening Space, embodied can also refer to a word that describes something that the explorer is **doing** (which includes their thinking). For example:

Procrastinating	*Prioritise*
Drive forwards	*Demonstrating*
Connecting with	*Shine*

If you find that your explorer uses an embodied word repeatedly, it may also be a clue that this word has significance for them.

The clues to choosing which words to repeat back when trying to establish the tethering post are therefore:

- Words that describe their **feelings**.
- Words that describe their **actions**.
- Embodied words that have been **repeated**.

Let's look at the examples taken from the three initial grazing responses in the previous section. I have emboldened the potential tethering posts and shown how they were offered back in each case (you may be able to find more). Each word or short phrase is offered as if asking a question, with a pause in-between. This gives the explorer time to notice how the different words 'land' for them.

Example 1:

Explorer: *Frustration.*
Facilitator: Frustration?

Example 2:

Explorer: *A feeling that I sometimes get when I feel my blood pressure is going up. Whether it's due to things that are going on at work, or the children, or anything else. I get that feeling of, not impending rage, but it just feels like things are getting to the **overload** stage. It feels like **pressure** inside my head.*

Facilitator: Overload?
Pressure?

Example 3:

Explorer: *The **fear of rejection** has been another component of what I want to connect to. I want to explore the notion of the fear of rejection, and then I might be able to see some connections to that. There certainly seems to me to be a limiting factor in what I do that I often don't go for things I should do because I have a sudden kind of **panic**. I definitely have a notion that the two are connected. The fear of rejection is like a skin of oil that **restricts** and **constricts** me; the more I try to **free myself**, the tighter it gets. It gets stronger as I try to fight it sometimes. It constricts me. It **covers** me. Increasingly it's not there. Sometimes I'm really **trapped** by it. Sometimes I'm not.*

So, I guess I'm not really sure what the two states are. Why should it be sometimes my fear gets initiated, sometimes it doesn't? It's not consistent.

Facilitator: Fear?

Fear of rejection?

Panic?

Restricts?

Constricts?

Free myself?

Covers?

Trapped?

Notice how repeating back words during this stage of the process (ie. *establishing* the tethering post) is done in the order that the words were said. It is as if you are following the explorer's story from where they began to where they left off.

If you're feeling uncertain about which words to repeat back, then just offer back whole phrases. Remember, so long as the words you repeat back are the explorer's words, you cannot go wrong.

What follows is an activity for you to get some practice in choosing which words to repeat back when inviting your explorer to choose a tethering post.

ACTIVITY: Establishing a Tethering Post

Below are some examples taken from the initial responses to asking:

What would you like to explore?

Have a go at choosing some embodied words to repeat back from each of these statements.

1. *I'm getting a slight feeling of holding in there.*
2. *I want to have a sense of ease around the day.*
3. *I'd really like to be noticing my breathing, how the breath comes through my nose into my lungs.*
4. *I pulled a muscle in the back of my hip. It's sore and aggravating. I've been very distracted by it lately.*
5. *I want to embody dancing through life connecting with the hearts and mind of others.*
6. *I'd like to clear the decks. I feel like I need a bit of a breathing space to get my attention on the job. I've got to lay things out that I need to do.*
7. *I want to go into the writing today with a sense of excitement.*
8. *I'm feeling pulled in too many directions.*
9. *I'm feeling very excited about this project. I know that they want me to connect with our stakeholders*
10. *I'm feeling stressed at the moment. This project could be critical to the survival of the company*

and my team are responsible for delivering on this. The different departments aren't working well together. I'm worried that we may fail.

Below are some possible options for embodied words to repeat back.

1. *I'm getting a **slight feeling of holding** in there.*
   Slight feeling of holding?
   Holding?
2. *I want to have a **sense of ease** around the day.*
   Sense of ease?
   Ease?
3. *I'd really like to be **noticing** my **breathing**, how the breath comes through my nose into my lungs.*
   Noticing?
   Breathing?
4. *I **pulled** a muscle in the back of my hip. It's **sore** and **aggravating**. I've been very **distracted** by it lately.*
   Pulled?
   Sore?
   Aggravating?
   Distracted
5. *I want to **embody dancing** through life **connecting** with the hearts and mind of others.*
   Embody dancing?
   Embody?
   Dancing?
   Connecting?

6. *I'd like to **clear the decks**. I feel like I need a bit of a **breathing space** to get **my attention** on the job. I've got to **lay things out** that I need to do.*
    Clear the decks?
    Breathing space?
    My attention?
    Lay things out?
7. *I want to **go into** the **writing** today with a **sense of excitement**.*
    Go into?
    Writing?
    Sense of excitement?
    Excitement?
8. *I'm **feeling pulled** in too many directions.*
    Feeling pulled?
    Pulled?
9. *I'm feeling very **excited** about this project. I know that they want me to **connect with** our stakeholders*
    Excited?
    Connect?
    Connect with?
10. *I'm **feeling stressed** at the moment. This project could be critical to the survival of the company and my team are responsible for delivering on this. The different departments aren't working well together. I'm **worried** that we may **fail**.*
    Feeling stressed?
    Stressed?
    Worried?
    Fail?

Establishing the tethering post is not a process to be rushed. Your explorer will appreciate being given time to connect with how they are feeling. The process of choosing may take a bit of teasing out. They may even want to hear the same words repeated back a few times. So be patient. With time, people almost always know when a particular word resonates for them – although this may seem hard to imagine until you have experienced this process for yourself (both as explorer and facilitator).

Occasionally, when trying to establish a tethering post, you might find that either:

- your explorer hasn't said anything that is obviously embodied; or
- none of the words that you have repeated back resonate for them in particular.

If this is the case, you can invite them to graze a little more by repeating back key words and asking:

Is there anything else about what you would like to explore?

Sooner or later they will settle on a focus word or short phrase that works for them. You will then be ready to move on to Step 3: exploring the tethering post.

Step 3: EXPLORING THE TETHERING POST

Once a tethering post has been established, you will be asking a specific set of questions that invite more in-depth exploration of the chosen focus word(s). Each time your explorer looks up from their grazing you will be bringing them back to the tethering post (x):

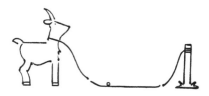

You do this by asking the questions in the order given below:

1. (And) **What kind of** 'x' is that?
2. (And) **Is there anything else about** 'x'?
3. (And) **Whereabouts is** 'x'?
4. (And) **Is 'x' on the inside or the outside**?*
5. (And) **Does** 'x' **have a size or a shape**?
6. (And) Does 'x' have a sound?**
7. (And) **Is there anything else** about 'x'?

Before each question, repeat back some of the words that your explorer has used.

You can repeat the final question (question 7):

---

* We have introduced the final of the five Clean questions here.
** This is the only question in this stage that is not one of David Grove's Clean questions.

> (And) **Is there anything else** about 'x'?

… until either:

- you are reaching the end of your agreed time; or
- the explorer says there is nothing more to say (although, it's not unusual for an explorer to say 'no', pause for thought, and then find they have more to say – so don't rush them).

I counted that I'd repeated the final question **Is there anything else about** 'x'? seven times in a recent facilitation – and the explorer hadn't even noticed!

This set of Clean questions are your way of saying, *Say some more about* 'x'? You will be helping to shine a **Clean Light of Attention** on the other person as they explore their inner experience.

There are some additional tips to consider when asking your questions:

i. Repeating back words

There is something very powerful about having someone bear witness to the words that you have spoken and hearing them repeated back to you. It creates a springboard for further thinking. Repeating back is perhaps the most important part of the process. You are acknowledging the fact that the words the explorer has chosen are important to them and you are helping them to listen to themselves.

Someone once shared with me their metaphor for repeating back another person's words, which I have found very helpful. I imagine that each word is like a pebble that the other person lays down between us. Some of these pebbles will be shiny, others dull, but each has a significance that only the explorer can know. I place some of the pebbles in the palm of my hand and gently wash them with my curiosity and respectful attention, brightening any flecks of interest or colour before offering them back. I try to make sure that I pause between words or phrases as I say them. It is as if I am savouring the words as I offer them back, rather than hurling them back in one go. This gives the explorer the chance to mull their words over as they receive them.

In this stage of the process (ie. *exploring* the tethering post) your repeating back should start with words or short phrases from the most recent response. You can also include words from previous responses. This helps to remind the explorer of all the aspects of their exploration, which can be particularly helpful as their exploration progresses.

It is best to limit your repeating back to a list of no more than four or five key words or short phrases before each question. Any more than this, and you are likely to distract your explorer with words rather than keeping them connected with their inner experience.

It can be tempting to favour the more positive thoughts and emotions in the words you repeat back. But remember that you have wiped your feet on the Welcome Mat. In a Listening Space we welcome and honour all thoughts and emotions in equal measure. We don't favour the comfortable over the uncomfortable, or vice versa.

As a facilitator, you do not need to repeat back every word your explorer says. In fact, a 'less is more' approach often works best. With your questions you can use a mix of:

- repeating key words only;
- repeating whole phrases or sentences; and
- asking a Clean question without any repeating back.

You can even make the words you repeat back into a question. For example, in response to:

Explorer: *It's like a big iron armour on the outside crushing inwards.*

… with an inquisitive tone of voice, you could say:

Facilitator: A big iron armour?
or
On the outside crushing inwards?

… and see if further thinking flows from this.

Repeating back the explorer's words has the added benefit of helping you to remember what they have said.

ii. Inviting metaphor

It is not unusual for a metaphor to appear, as if from nowhere, when you are exploring the tethering post. The metaphor creates a kind of 'thing-ness', or tangible form, to the embodied experience that is being explored. The three Clean questions that encourage metaphor to emerge in this way are:

(And) **Whereabouts is** 'x'?
(And) **Is** 'x' **on the inside or the outside**?
(And) **Does** 'x' **have a size or a shape**?

If a metaphor does appear, it helps if you favour the metaphoric words when you are repeating back. Here's an example:

Explorer: *I feel derailed. Like a train that's come off the tracks. I'm the carriage and I've just realised there's no engine.*

Not too difficult to spot the metaphor here!

Facilitator: Derailed.
A train that's come off the tracks.
A carriage.
And no engine.

Favouring the metaphoric words and bringing the explorer back to the tethering post each time encourages more details of the metaphor to come to the fore, helping to make it more vivid and memorable. The key is to spot the metaphor as it arises. But if you fail to spot it, don't worry – your explorer will likely as not refer to it again if it is important to them.

Having asked these questions in the order given, you may find a metaphor reveals itself and you may not. Either way is fine. The important thing is that your exploring goat is free to graze in whichever direction they choose, free from any pressure to find solutions or come up with a metaphor. They will appreciate having the space to be listened to with a quality of attention that is a rare treat in our busy and frenetic lives.

iii. Does 'x' have a sound
This question has recently been added to the Listening Space process at the suggestion of a musician friend[19] of mine. Whilst this is not a Clean question, it often generates some useful insights.

However, it is best not to try and repeat back the sound itself that the explorer makes, as it could sound like you are mimicking. Instead, repeat back the words that *describe* the sound. For example:

Humming	*Joyous sound*
Crashing	*Boom*
Singing	*Roar*

iv. 'So' or 'And'
You may be wondering why each question has the option of starting with *'And'*, since this is not what happens in general conversation. *'And'* has the effect of acknowledging what has already been said and gives a sense of continuation with what

---

19. Thank you Ruth Huckle.

will be said next. '*So*' would probably be the more conversational thing to say but sounds more abrupt and can imply some kind of judgement.

It can also sound gentler to use '*and*' when you are repeating back words. Here's an example for you:

Explorer: *There's a feeling of tension all around the top half of my body. It's trying to stay in control that's creating it.*
Facilitator: And a feeling of tension.
              And trying to stay in control.
              And **is there anything else about** tension?

You can experiment with using '*and*' at times, and not at others.

v. Drawing a blank

If at any point your questions draw a blank, or the explorer looks at you in confusion, then calmly repeat back some key words and move on to the next question.

For example, your explorer might find it difficult to answer;

(And) **Whereabouts is** 'x'?

... especially if they are not familiar with noticing what is happening in their body. They might not be able to identify a location for their focus word: for example – *frustrated, ease, empty* or *hopeful*.

If they answer '*I don't know*' or '*What do you mean, where is it?*' – or simply look at you as if you've lost the plot – then move on to your next question:

(And) **Is 'x' on the inside or the outside?**

This question is usually enough of a clue that you are asking them to notice what is happening in or around their body.

If again they have no answer, then again move on and ask the next questions:

(And) **Does 'x' have a size or a shape?**
(And) Does 'x' have a sound?

The key is to ask each question with confidence and assume that your explorer will know the answer – and not to be fazed if they don't!

vi. When asking the question seems counterintuitive

If you have asked the first two questions and your explorer has already mentioned where the feeling is, and perhaps even suggested a shape:

It's like a balloon filling my chest.

… it might seem counter-intuitive to ask the next three questions:

(And) **Whereabouts is** 'x'?
(And) **Is** 'x' **on the inside or the outside?**
(And) **Does** 'x' **have a size or a shape?**

However, these questions invite a person to connect a little more deeply with their inner experience and can bring unexpected answers. So, don't be tempted to leave them out.

Step 4: CREATING AN IMAGE

Ask your explorer if they would like to represent what they have discovered on paper in some way. Invite them to use coloured pens/pencils if they would like.

If they look a little uncertain, you can gently encourage them by saying something like:

It might be that you create an image or diagram.
Or perhaps a mind-map.
You don't have to show anyone what you have drawn or written.
And if nothing comes to mind, that's fine.

If your explorer chooses not to draw anything, then you can move straight on to Step 6.

Step 5: EXPLORING THE IMAGE

Encourage your explorer to reflect on what they have drawn by asking the following questions:

> What do you notice as you look at the image you have created?
> **Is there anything else about** what you notice?

Give them time to notice what arises for them as they examine the image they have created. At this stage there is no need to repeat back their words. The image itself holds much of the information they will be discovering about themselves and your words could be a distraction.

Finally, resist any temptation to comment on, or ask questions about, what they have drawn; remember you are shining a Clean Light of Attention on your explorer.

Step 6: ENDING THE SESSION

To end the session, invite your explorer to reflect on what they have gleaned from their grazing by asking:

> What do you know now about 'x'?
> And what difference does knowing that make?

You can then gently invite them to leave their field of grazing by saying:

And would that be an OK place to leave it?

Again, it is best not to repeat back words at this final stage of the session. These questions are an invitation to round off their thinking in a way that works for them. They may leave with problems unresolved and ideas half-formed. Remember, it is not your job to fix things or help them find solutions.

From start to finish, a Listening Space usually lasts about 20 minutes. But the length of each session can vary greatly – and that's fine. Some people need to say more, others less.

Very often, further thinking happens after the session. As one explorer explained to me, she found herself thinking intensively for a week or so about the feeling of *'empty'* that was the tethering post for her Listening Space. Whilst this wasn't a comfortable feeling for her, she gained some very useful insights and a more resourceful perspective over time.

There is a summary of the questions and instructions needed to hold a Listening Space on the following pages. Most people find it helpful to have this in front of them when they are facilitating someone. It leaves them free to place their attention on their explorer rather than worrying about what question to ask next. With practice the questions will become familiar and, over time, you may find it helpful to learn them by heart.

SUMMARY OF QUESTIONS FOR CREATING A LISTENING SPACE

1. STARTING THE SESSION

What would you like to explore?

2. ESTABLISHING THE TETHERING POST (x)

I'm going to repeat back some of your words.
Let me know which word or short phrase resonates most for you.
This will become the focus word (or phrase).

3. EXPLORING THE TETHERING POST (x)

Repeat back key words before asking:

1. (And) **What kind of** 'x' is that?
2. (And) **Is there anything else about** 'x'?
3. (And) **Whereabouts is** 'x'?
4. (And) **Is** 'x' **on the inside or the outside?**
5. (And) **Does** 'x' **have a size or a shape?**
6. (And) Does 'x' have a sound?
7. (And) **Is there anything else about** 'x'?

[Question 7 can be repeated until there is no more to say]

4. CREATING AN IMAGE

Would you like to represent what you have discovered on paper in some way?
You may want to use coloured pens/pencils.

5. EXPLORING THE IMAGE

What do you notice as you look at the image you have created?
Is there anything else about what you notice?

6. ENDING THE SESSION

What do you know now about 'x'?
And what difference does knowing that make?
And would that be an OK place to leave it?

At the end of each session, I invite the explorer to continue noticing what arises for them over time. The emphasis is on the **noticing** rather than trying to change things. So often, change happens naturally when we gain awareness and acceptance of our inner experience. I encourage them to revisit the image that they have created over the coming weeks (and beyond) and ask themselves:

> What am I noticing now?
> **Is there anything else about** what I'm noticing?

They may find that further thoughts arise for them or that they want to create a new, updated image that captures any fresh insights they have gained.

Remember the quote from my friend:

> *Metaphor creates the starting point for a story.*
> *When a metaphor comes to your mind you can ask yourself:*
> *How will I use this to move forward in my story?*

You could even invite your explorer to ask themselves this question:

> How will I use this to move forward in my story?

GENERAL HANDY HINTS

The power of the Listening Space comes from following this six-step structure. Although it may seem restrictive at first to ask the questions in this prescriptive way, don't be tempted to deviate from the process and add comments or additional questions that you feel might benefit the explorer. Most explorers find it very liberating to be given the opportunity to think for themselves in this way. You may just have to trust the process until you have had a chance to be both facilitator and explorer a few times. The best way to learn about a Listening Space is to experience it for yourself. People are complex beings and the simplicity of the questions and overall process allows space for that complexity to emerge.

There are, however, some handy hints that will help to make you even more effective in the way you facilitate a Listening Space.

i. A sense of ease

It helps if you can bring a sense of ease to your listening. Give a reassuring nod from time to time. An encouraging *oh, ahh,* or *hmm.* Maybe a smile too. Let go of the need to 'get somewhere'. It is as if you are puzzling things out and discovering things together.

You may have to sit with the discomfort of uncertainty, of not knowing where the explorer's thinking will take them. Just sit back and be curious. Give them your undivided attention. Trust that things will unfold as they need to. Be patient and open to the possibility of change happening spontaneously as your explorer gains fresh insights and information. Ironically, the less you try to help, the more things are likely to change of their own accord. As I mentioned earlier, since the explorer is free to decide which direction to take in their exploration, any ideas or solutions they arrive at are likely to be a best fit for them.

Sometimes you might find that your explorer gets upset, which can feel unsettling. Remember that you are giving them a space for wholehearted exploration. If you stay calm and welcome all thoughts and emotions in equal measure, it will help to reassure the explorer that they don't need to be afraid of difficult emotions. And they don't need to censor things to make you feel comfortable.

ii. Your tone of voice

It helps to have some variation in your tone of voice as you repeat back words and ask your questions. You might, for example, want to sound supportive, playful, challenging, or even gently teasing – all the while being curious. There will be times when sounding conversational and upbeat is more appropriate. And other times when you might want to slow the delivery of your words down. If you notice the explorer becoming deeply connected with their inner experience, you can become almost hypnotic in your tone of voice.

Experiment with using your intonation in a way that makes your Listening Space a warm, friendly and safe place for exploring. What's important is that you use your tone of voice in a way that feels authentic for you.

Finally, avoid sounding sorry for your explorer if they talk about things that are difficult for them. Rather, repeat back key words as if you are mulling over what they have said with curiosity.

iii. Eye contact

In a Listening Space you might start by having eye contact. However, it is helpful if you can bring your gaze to the things that your explorer is noticing in or around their body as the session progresses. In doing so you encourage them to connect with their inner experience, rather than connecting with you.

This is contrary to what we are taught about 'good' listening, where we are told that maintaining eye contact is important. It is perhaps worth reassuring yourself that some of our most 'connected' conversations happen when eye contact is not possible: whilst out on a walk together; sitting beside someone when driving; or when talking on the telephone.

iv. Your gestures

If you are facilitating someone face-to-face, or online with video, then it is useful to pay attention to your explorer's gestures. People will often gesture or gaze towards the things that they are talking about, especially when a metaphor appears. For example, they may show with their hands where the metaphoric armour exists around the top half of their body or look down to the key that has appeared in the keyhole in the middle of their chest.

Try to imagine that these things really exist in the physical space in which your explorer is experiencing them. Direct your words and your gaze towards the metaphor as it arises and gently gesture to it as you repeat back their words and ask your questions. This means that when your explorer talks about a keyhole that is in the front of their chest, you gesture to their chest and not yours. Subtle gesturing in this way helps to acknowledge and honour the explorer's metaphors and keeps them engaged with their own experience.

v. Being precise

As much as is possible, repeat back the exact words that the explorer has used. For example, if they refer to '*tension*', then this is the word that you use – not '*tensing*', '*feeling tense*', or some other variation which you feel has the same meaning.

This means that Clean questions are not always grammatically correct, and they can seem slightly strange to ask to begin with. However, given a bit of practice, you will soon get used to them and you can be assured that the person receiving the question rarely hears them as odd. Quite the opposite, most people say they feel like they've been truly heard and understood when they are given the space to explore their own thinking in this way.

vi. Keeping track

To aid my memory I find it helpful to write down the explorer's words as we go along. I've never known an explorer to be distracted by the fact that I am writing and they often like to take a copy to read back over after the session. Alternatively, you might find you listen better if you put your pen and paper down. You can experiment to see what works best for you.

What follows is an example of the notes I made during the Listening Space session that is shared later in this chapter.

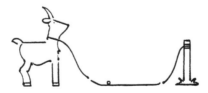

A good father.
Same amount attention love.

Personalities very different
Eldest regularly complains — favour the younger
Easier to connect with the younger
More extrovert

Engage with him — respond to him
Right balance
Approach this in a way that is fair

FAIR

Doesn't necessarily need same amount of attention
Conveys that I love them both
Equally
Individually 100%
Not a divided love
Not about division

Communicate to both that I love them each 100%

Happy that he expresses his concern
Find a way to let him realise I love them equally

Heart opening
Flower with petals
Flowery energy

Important value
Complaints understandable
More and more urgent
Needs to be addressed now

Lack of experience — hindering me
Not sure what's natural — normal or extreme
Negotiator
Help them make peace

Find a way of expressing my love — understands as
love
Too reactive
Waiting for them to come to me
Flower willing to open up to the suns
Younger son taller — standing closer
Older son a bit held back

Open and vulnerable
Express my love more without waiting for them to come
and get it
More proactive
More responsible — more empowered
It's up to me to do something about this.

vii. Keeping it all about the explorer

Avoid the temptation to use phrases like:

Tell me about … ?
What I'm hearing you say is …
What I think you're saying is …
I get the feeling that …
My sense is that …

Using these phrases has the effect of making the explorer shift their attention from their own experience to you. Remember, the purpose of the Listening Space is to encourage them to stay engaged with their own exploration rather than being concerned about your understanding of the words they have used.

viii. Changing pronouns

Whilst most of the time you will be repeating back the explorer's exact words, as a general rule when they say *'I'* or *'my'* it sounds more natural if you repeat this back as *'you'* or *'your'*. For example, if they say:

*I feel tension in **my** belly.*

you might ask:

Whereabouts in **your** belly?

There is, however, one exception to this general rule. Occasionally, your explorer might say *'I'* or *'my'* as one of their focus words when you are establishing a tethering post.

For example:

My healing.
Whole me.
My love.

In this instance, it works best if you keep the pronoun as it is, rather than changing it to *'you'* or *'your'*. For example, *'my healing'*, stays as it is; it is **not** changed to *'your healing'*.

ix. Being flexible

As you have seen, the Listening Space is a structured process with rules to follow. The more you practice the process, the more you will come to appreciate the power of the simplicity of the questions.

However, as with any process, the unexpected can happen and you may need to demonstrate some flexibility. For example, someone recently shared with me her story of holding a Listening Space for a friend. After asking the opening question, *'What would you like to explore?'*, her friend talked about some deeply personal issues for over an hour. When he finally looked up from his grazing he said, *'I haven't talked about these things since I was a teenager'* (he is now in his sixties). They ran out of time before ever reaching the stage of establishing a tethering post! It seems that we should never underestimate the impact of simply listening to another person with our full attention.

x. Coming to the body

Since this process is all about inviting your explorer to connect with their inner experience, it can be really helpful to start your Listening Space with the Clean Breathing Meditation that was introduced on p54 of the ground floor room, **Being With Yourself**. You might like to read this script out before you begin your questions.

AFTER THE SESSION

It is essential to ensure that what is said in the Listening Space stays in the Listening Space, unless the explorer chooses otherwise. Even after the session has finished we must remember that in this Lighthouse of Mindful Exploration we need to let go of the desire to analyse, fix or judge. Wiping your feet on the Welcome Mat helps you avoid the temptation of going into Rescuer role, especially if the explorer has talked about something that distresses them. A well-intended comment like …

Thank you so much for sharing that.
That must have been so difficult for you.

… can inadvertently put the explorer into the role of Victim. Remember, we are shining a Clean Light of Attention on the explorer, and it is not for us to know what is or isn't difficult for them.

You will also need to resist the temptation to comment on any metaphors that arise (however fascinating you might find them). Our metaphors can have deeply personal significance for us and it can feel very intrusive if others discuss or analyse them without our permission.

As I mentioned earlier, people often continue to process their thinking well after the Listening Space has finished. They may gain fresh insights and arrive at new solutions to the problems that they face. There are some different ways to increase the chances of this happening. Your explorer may find it helpful to carry out one or two of them after the session:

Mind-mapping: they may want to create a mind-map of key words or phrases they have used.

Researching words: looking up key words in a dictionary or etymology dictionary may shed a new light on the meaning of their words.

Researching metaphors: there are various books and online resources available for researching the symbolic significance of any metaphors that arise during a session. This often reveals additional layers of information and generates a deeper level of understanding.

Creating an image: although this is an integral part of the process, your explorer might like to create further images to represent what they have discovered. This is an opportunity to have fun with pens, paint, photography, collaging or searching for images online.

Creating a scrapbook or sketchbook: some people like to create a scrapbook, sketchbook, or folder for safekeeping of the images that they create. It provides a way being able to review what they have discovered about themselves over time – almost like a personal storybook.

Creating a model: your explorer may want to get creative and represent their metaphor with clay, Plasticine, Lego, or some other 3D modelling material.

Creating a sound: some explorers like to find creative expression through sound or music.

Creating a movement: or maybe movement and dance is their thing.

Visiting places: you could even invite them to visit a place that represents the metaphors that arose for them – such as the lighthouse of this book.

A LISTENING SPACE STORY TO SHARE

The metaphors that we naturally use are a great way of bringing mindful awareness to our inner experience. They give us useful insights, reveal solutions that were previously hidden from view, and help us to develop a different relationship with the challenges that we face. This is beautifully illustrated by the story that follows, taken from a Listening Space session in which a father explores his relationship with his two sons (my questions are in bold).

So, what would you like to explore?

I have two sons, 11 and 13 years old, who live with me some of the time.

I'm very keen to be a good father to them – to give them both the same amount of attention, of love. But their personalities are very different, and my eldest regularly complains that I favour the younger one. Which I'm sure I don't.

However, it is easier for me to connect with my younger son because he's more of an extrovert. He is always inviting me to engage with him, to respond to him.

So now I'm looking for the right balance. How can I approach this in a way that is fair, that they both realise that I care for them fully, without giving more to one than the other?

A good father.
Connect with.
The same amount of attention.
The right balance.
Fair.
Care for them fully.
Do any of these words resonate for you in particular?
I noticed something happening inside me when you said 'fair'. Fair seems to be a very, very important thing to me.

What kind of fair is that?
It's a fair that doesn't necessarily need the same amount of attention to both of them, in time or energy, but still conveys that I love them both equally. Equally isn't even the right word because I love them both individually one hundred percent. So, it's not a divided love, where both get fifty percent. In this case fair is not about division. It's more about being able to communicate to both that I love them each one hundred percent, even if I engage with one more than the other.

It's not a divided love.
And communicate to both that you love them one hundred percent.

And is there anything else about fair?

Well, I know I'm being fair, but I'm not sure that the eldest gets it. I'm very happy that he expresses his concern about me favouring his brother, but I would like to find a way to let him realise that I love them equally.

Happy that he does express his concern.
And how can you approach this.
And whereabouts is fair, like that?

Notice how words from previous responses have been included in the repeating back to help to remind the explorer of other aspects of his exploration.

When you asked that question I had a feeling of my heart opening, like a flower with petals, opening.

Is fair on the inside or the outside?

It's on the outside, in front of my chest.

And does fair have a size or a shape?

It's about the size of a DVD. And it's like a flower. Not like a real, material flower. It's like a flowery energy.

A flowery energy, in front of your chest.
And is there anything else about fair?

I had hoped that it was obvious to both of them that I love them equally because it's obvious to me. Being fair is a very important value to me, in a broader sense. I can be very annoyed, rebellious, angry even, when things aren't fair. Which makes the complaints of my eldest son very understandable to me. It resonates. That's why it feels like a problem that I really need to sort out. To me it's fair, but he doesn't perceive it as such.

And, as I'm talking about this, I realise it's getting more and more urgent. It needs to be addressed now.

More and more urgent.
It needs to be addressed now.
And a flowery energy.
And is there anything else about fair?

Well what comes up is that I was an only child, so the whole issue of fair, in this sense, never came up in my own childhood. I never had to quarrel, for example. And what I'm thinking is that maybe my own lack of experience of having siblings might be hindering me in dealing with this. I'm not sure what's natural and what isn't, what's normal or extreme.

It might be tempting at times to add words of reassurance when you are listening to someone – *I'm sure they do know that you love them really*. But in a Listening Space, your curious and welcoming attention is all the reassurance that is needed.

They tend to fight a lot, my boys. Not in a very extreme way, but they do. My first inclination is always to be a negotiator and help them make peace. But their mother always says to me, 'Let them be. They're boys, they'll work it out.'

You're not sure what's normal or extreme.
And love them equally.
Is there anything else about fair?

No, not really, I just need to find a way of expressing my love to my eldest that he understands as love. And perhaps I am too reactive, waiting for them to come to me - which turns out to be a lot easier for the youngest one to do.

I then invited him to represent what he had explored on paper in some way, and this is what he drew:

I asked:

What do you notice as you look at the image you have created?
I've drawn a flower opening up (that's me) and two suns – sons and suns! I'm like a flower willing to open up to the suns.
What really strikes me as I look at this is that I'm lucky they are so near to each other. It makes it possible for me to direct my attention to both of them. If they had been on either side of me, I'd have struggled to open out to them both. So that's a relief.
The other thing I notice is that, without intending to, I have drawn the younger son taller than his brother, and it looks like he is standing closer to me. In reality my eldest son is taller than me, and his younger brother shorter ... Very weird! In a sense it

describes what I was talking about, of course. My older son is a bit held back. And the younger is inclined to come forward, to be more present, to let everybody know that he's there.

Is there anything else about what you notice?
I look a bit flabbergasted, like someone who doesn't really know what to do.
But as a whole I'm rather open and able to be vulnerable.

And what do you know now about fair?
That there's a difference between feeling the same amount of love for both of them and showing it. Perhaps I should express my love more without waiting for them to come and get it, to come and get the attention.

And what difference does knowing that make?
I think I should be more proactive in this. I feel more responsible for what's going on. At the same time, I feel more empowered. Most of all, it's up to me to do something about this.

Notice how a metaphor seemed to appear from nowhere: a flowery energy in front of his chest. It became the starting point for a story that seemed to unfold in front of our eyes, revealing a solution that was a perfect fit for this individual: expressing his love rather than waiting for his sons to come and get it. Whilst a Listening Space does not always involve metaphor, this kind of thing happens time and again when people are asked Clean questions in this way.

I asked him to reflect on what his experience of this Listening Space had been:

Wonderful actually!

I keep being amazed by how good it feels to hear your own words repeated back to you. It's helped me to get in touch with what's going on inside of me.

Like when we were exploring what the right focus word should be; you gave back the word 'fair' and immediately something happened inside me, which hadn't happened as I was saying it. It's close to miraculous.

What I also liked was the persistence in repeating the same question over and over. I was surprised by just how much information was available. More than would come to mind in the first place.

(The notes that were taken during this Listening Space have already been shown on p161-2)

In a follow-up email a few weeks after this session, this father-of-two reflected on what he had noticed since his Listening Space:

When I saw the boys again the atmosphere was very relaxed, more relaxed than usual. Although I didn't do anything specific to bring that about.

And there was something I noticed about the drawing that I had made. As I looked at it two days after our session, something struck me as odd. I liked the son/sun pun, but things seemed reversed. I realised it would be much more appropriate if I were the sun (one instead of two) and the boys would be the flowers. A sun gives it's light and warmth indiscriminately; there would be more than enough for both flowers,

What this shows me is that up until now I was probably more

concerned with receiving love from them than giving love to them.

I have adjusted the image in my head. I am now that sun, giving light and warmth to the flowers.

Even after the session this father's metaphor produced insights that had a transformative effect on his relationship with his sons. As so often happens, the metaphor became a gift that kept giving.

So now you have the process from start to finish. If you'd like to see recordings of a Listening Space session you can visit www.thelisteningspace.co.uk/the-listening-space.

YOUR TURN NOW

It's your turn now. You might want to find a practice partner and create a whole Listening Space for one another.

Remember that this does not need to be done face-to-face, and you can have the questions on p154-5 in front of you rather than having to remember them.

For most people, holding a Listening Space for someone takes a bit of getting used to. The questions may seem a little wooden at first and it can feel rather daunting to set aside the desire to 'fix'. Some people find they can relax easily into asking questions in this way, whilst others take a little longer. A bit of practice is usually all that is needed. Just be patient with yourself as you have a go. You will find the questions get easier with use, so don't give up if they do seem unfamiliar.

Remember that, although the process is prescriptive, it can also be very liberating. As an explorer you are given the freedom to think for yourself. As a facilitator you are freed from having to think about what questions to ask next. Instead, you can bring greater awareness to your way of 'being', your presence, as you shine the light of your attention on your explorer. You can follow your intuition in the way that you use:

- your body language and your gestures;
- your facial expression;
- your eye gaze and eye contact; and
- your intonation.

If you're concerned about remembering the words that your explorer gives in answer to your questions, then bear in mind that:

- you can write the words down as you go along;
- you will be able to give your full attention to the words they are using rather than getting distracted about what your response or advice will be;
- you don't need to remember whole sentences – it is more effective to just use key words to prompt the explorer's thinking; and
- any metaphors that do arise tend to be memorable in themselves – especially if you try to picture in your own mind what the explorer is describing.

All these things help to reduce the mental effort involved in remembering so that you can bring a sense of ease as you listen with careful attention.

Being listened to with the quality of attention that is generated in a Listening Space is a rare treat. Enjoy!

ACTIVITY: Creating Your Own Listening Space

Decide who will be facilitator and who will be explorer. You will both need a pen and paper.
The explorer may also like to have coloured pens/pencils to hand.

Remember that before you begin you will need to:

- make sure that you have mutual agreement;
- set a time frame;
- establish confidentiality; and
- give a brief description of what is involved if your explorer is new to the process.

The facilitator can use the questions on p154-5 to guide them as they:

- start the session;
- establish a tethering post;
- use repeating back and Clean questions to encourage exploration, which may or may not be through metaphor;
- invite the explorer to create and explore an image; and
- bring the session to a close.

Once you have completed the process, swap roles and compare experiences.

What did you notice?
- What did you notice as a facilitator?
- And as an explorer?

Holding a Listening Space for someone else is, in my experience, a real privilege. Being witness to the stories as they emerge can be a real source of wonder and fascination. I invariably learn something from what has been said.

Equally, being on the receiving end of a Listening Space is a very nourishing, calming experience in which I often do my best thinking.

Here are some comments that others have shared with me about their experience of being an **explorer**:

I liked that you were acknowledging everything. I could feel myself going 'yep, yep, yep' inside as you repeated back my words. It also helped me unpick what was going on for me.

I felt very listened to. It was very freeing to be able to put my attention where I wanted it to go and I could relax in the knowledge that I'd always be brought back to the focus word.

I ended up talking about a problem, but the more I explored it the less of a problem it became.

The questions helped me dig deeper to get to the next layer of thoughts and emotions.

Sometimes it's as if my thoughts are written on shredded paper in the shape of a brain. The thoughts are all scrambled up and make me doubt what I'm doing. Clean questions help me unscramble my thoughts by putting the shredded paper into piles and ordering the strands of thinking.

A metaphor seemed to come to me out of nowhere. It was like I was that tree in the middle of the field. It made my situation seem less threatening because I was talking about the tree instead of me. The more I explored the tree the more I learnt about my situation. It felt safer to be able to talk about things in this way. I didn't have to go into all the detail of what had happened.

And of being a **facilitator**:

I didn't have to worry about where I should go next with my questions because I knew I would keep bringing the explorer back to the focus word. It meant I could relax and hear more.

I found it really difficult to let go of wanting to make things better for them at first. But I now find it very reassuring to know that I'm not there to help fix things and everything that they say is OK. It stays in the Listening Space and I don't have to be burdened with it afterwards.

If you would like to be supported in learning this process, then you might like to join one of the Listening Space courses.

Visit *www.thelisteningspace.co.uk/courses* to find out more.

Summary

I hope you have enjoyed the process of learning to create a Listening Space, both as a facilitator and an explorer. You may already have identified ways in which using this process could be of value in your work or personal life.

If you climb with me to the top floor, ***The Lantern Room***, you might get some more ideas about the ways in which you could use Clean questions and the Listening Space in your everyday life.

Chapter 5

The Lantern Room

People shine not in the glow of your charisma.
They shine in the light of your attention for them...
They shine when you remind them that they matter.

Nancy Kline, *Time to Think*

Welcome to ***The Lantern Room***, the very top of this **Lighthouse of Mindful Exploration**, where we will be taking a look at some of the ways that we can bring what has been learnt on our way up the building out into our everyday lives. But before we do so let's just recap on our journey so far.

After wiping our feet on the **Welcome Mat** to remove any desire to fix, change, or judge ourselves or others, we used the **Key of Curiosity** to open the door to a mindset of open-minded enquiry.

We familiarised ourselves with the Clean questions contained within the **Clean Bricks** from which the building is constructed. The rules for using this specific set of questions are straightforward: use only the words or phrases that the other person has used along with a Clean question. This is our tool for maintaining a 'Clean mindset', since we are prevented from making suggestions or analysing what the other person says or does. Rather than fitting people into predetermined categories or neatly labelled boxes, we give them the space to figure themselves out.

Clean questions involve listening at two levels:

- First, the person asking the questions must listen with careful attention in order to repeat back words or phrases that the other person has used.
- Second, the person answering gets to listen to themselves as they hear their words repeated back.

There is something very powerful about having someone act as companion to our exploration and bear witness to our thinking in this way. It gives us the space to connect with what feels right for us in the decisions we make.

It is a 'Clean mindset' which creates the beam of light that is emitted from the Lantern Room. The beam is broad, ranging from:

- simply doing an internal 'press pause' to notice the

story we are telling ourselves about a situation; to
- asking one or two Clean questions in general conversation; to
- using a Listening Space for more in-depth exploration.

The beam is also far-reaching, since Clean exploration can be used in a range of different contexts:

- Gathering information.
- Exploring problems.
- Exploring solutions.
- Generating new and creative ideas.

We can even ask these questions of ourselves.

When we ask Clean questions of others we invite them to expand on what they have said without contaminating the interaction with our own assumptions and interpretations. This enables us to check out how closely our understanding of what the other person has said matches the meaning they are trying to convey, so avoiding or overcoming misunderstandings.

When we ask Clean questions of ourselves we become more aware of our own experience. This was our focus on the ground floor, ***Being With Yourself***, where we used Clean questions to help tune in to the various aspects of our experience as we visited each of the seven brightly coloured **Rainbow Beanbag Cushions** – representing our five senses, our thoughts and our emotions.

We were encouraged to become curious about how things 'actually' are rather than judging ourselves or others when things aren't the way we feel they 'ought' to be. We were invited to accept the whole range of our thoughts and emotions and remove the metaphoric armour we wear to protect ourselves from vulnerability:

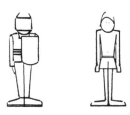

- Our **Flak Jacket of Perfection** that keeps us pretending to be the person we feel we 'should' be in order to fend off criticism.
- Our **Shield of Safety** that we might hold up as a barrier to engaging in relationships, thus avoiding the risk of failure, rejection and loss. It also shields us from engaging in personal or work projects.
- Our helmet with its **Visor of Certainty** that makes us view things in a way that fits with our model of how the world works, convincing us that we have the 'right' way of seeing things.

We took notice of the thoughts and emotions that we generate from the evidence we get from our senses, and saw how we create meaning from situations that may or may not be the reality. We learnt how becoming an observer of our own experience helps to prevent us getting swept up in our usual emotional responses to what is happening. If we pause and allow each moment to be exactly as it is, and ourselves to be exactly as we are, we come to see our situation with greater clarity. Different perspectives and choices reveal themselves.

As a way of gaining further insights about our thinking, we were introduced to the drama roles that we tend to play when situations aren't going the way we would like them to:

- **Persecutor** – pointing the finger of blame at others.
- **Victim** – with feelings of inadequacy and helplessness.
- **Rescuer** – with a desire to make things better for others.

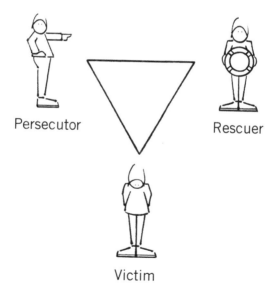

Persecutor

Rescuer

Victim

When we are listening to others it is easy to find ourselves slipping 'into drama'. We may feel pulled to make things better or frustrated that the other person isn't sorting themselves out. There may be times that the things the other person says trigger uncomfortable feelings for us. At these moments it may be helpful to inwardly acknowledge our own experience with compassion and remind ourselves that it is not our role in this lighthouse to fix or judge. Rather we are giving the person the freedom to explore his or her own thoughts and emotions. This is why we spent time listening to ourselves before turning our attention to listening to others higher up the building.

Moving up to the first floor, **The Room of Metaphor**, we saw how metaphor – describing one thing in terms of another – captures the essence of our experience in a way that is more tangible. Exploring the metaphors that we naturally use to describe our experience can be a very powerful way of coming to know ourselves and others better.

On the second floor, **Being With Others**, we learnt how to ask Clean questions in a more structured way to create a Listening Space for someone else. We imagined this person – the explorer – to be like a tethered goat grazing freely around a particular issue, only looking up when they are ready for our next question. Each time they look up, we use a combination of repeating back key words and asking a Clean question to bring them back to the tethering post. In doing so, we bring the focus of their attention back to their inner experience each time.

We learnt how to ask our questions in a way that encourages metaphors to emerge and develop, bringing an almost magical quality to the explorer's thinking.

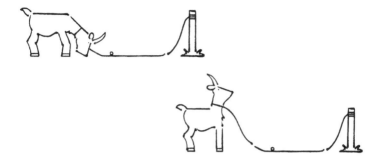

Which brings us up to where we are now, **_The Lantern Room_**.

The Lantern Room

The light that is emitted from the top floor of this lighthouse is created from Clean exploration – a combination of careful listening, repeating back the words a person has used and asking Clean questions. In this room we will consider how shining a **Clean Light of Attention** on ourselves and others can help to:

- gain clarity on which direction to take next;
- navigate the rocks and storms in life; and
- notice the beauty in the surrounding landscape.

At this point I would like to introduce you to seven people from very different walks of life who each have their stories to tell about the ways in which they have been bringing Clean exploration into their everyday lives. Their names have been changed in order to protect their identities. What follows is a series of interviews with each of these individuals in which I asked them the following question:

What impact has learning about Clean exploration had for you?

Sophie

Meet Sophie. She is a mother of two young children; Ella, who is eight years old, and Sam, who is five. She had been finding herself getting run down by all the demands of raising a young family and was looking for more constructive ways of managing her children's more challenging behaviour. She came across Clean questions at a parent workshop:

What impact has learning about Clean exploration had for you?

It had an impact from the word go. After the first parent session I came to, I remember picking Sam up from nursery and I was asking him the usual round of questions:

Did you have a nice day today?
What things did you do?
Who did you play with?

And I got the typical few words in response:

I don't know.
Nothing.
I don't remember.

And then he said:

Oh, we had a snack.

I thought I knew everything about snack time, but I paused and thought I'd just ask a Clean question:

What kind of snack?

And he told me about the snack. So I carried on:

> **Me:** **Is there anything else about** that snack?
> **Sam:** *Oh, and I sat next to Ben, and he didn't like it, but I really did.*
> **Me:** And **is there anything else?**

I found out all this stuff about a part of his day that was quite a highlight for him. He just volunteered the information. So I guess the first thing I noticed is that these questions are a good way of getting information out of the kids in a way that didn't feel nosey. They can tell me their story and I learn about what is going on for them. I get more insight into what it's like being them – which I love.

I've also used Clean questions to help me know how to help them. For example, Ella has always found it really hard walking into a busy playground and getting to school two minutes before the doors open. There are lots things that could have been making her distressed – noise, space, anticipation, saying goodbye to me – and I'd never really got to the bottom of it. If you don't know what's hard about a situation then it's difficult to know how to fix it.

So I sat down on my bed with her and asked her if it was OK to try and find out what was going on. I asked a few Clean questions about going into the playground and she came up with this brilliant metaphor:

It's like walking into a room where a bomb of children has just gone off.

I suddenly understood that there was a really big impact and disorder for her that was to do with the noisiness and the movement. She kept doing this gesture exploding up and out with her hands, which seemed really significant for her. I discovered that her distress wasn't so much about saying goodbye to me or about being nervous at school, it was about dealing with the sensory overload – that bomb of children. So now we make sure we get to school when it's quieter. She's fine if she's already there and things build up as people come in – she can absorb that. But walking into a space that's already full is hard for her.

Everyone had always said, *'She's just clingy. She just needs to get used to it.'* But you can't get used to bombs going off. If that's how it feels then it's not something that you should have to get used to. Clean questions gave meaningful depth to her experience – it let me separate the issues out rather than just assuming that it was because she was clingy.

Clean has helped me realise how much the way my thinking colours the way I see things. I'm much more aware now that I am not other people and they are not me – which sounds very obvious, but it's easy to forget that not everybody is thinking or feeling what I'm thinking or feeling. You only have to realise that once and then it has a profound effect forever.

Is there anything else?

Yes. I used to get these awful headaches every morning at about half past ten. The doctor said I had chronic migraine and I was prescribed some strong medication, which I really didn't want to take. I was thinking about the pain and started asking myself some Clean questions about it:

> **What kind of** pain was it?
> **Whereabouts** was it?
> **Was there anything else about** that pain?
> **Did it have a size or a shape?**

I realised that I was embodying my distress at having to keep sending Ella to school – this was where I held everything in. I was making her do this thing that was really hurting her and, as a result, I was hurting myself. It was really bizarre because my headaches went away almost instantaneously as soon as I realised I was processing things in this way. I still felt really bad but it stopped being something that I didn't have any control over. It started being something that I could change.

It's made me realise a lot about the way I embody things. I do it all the time and it's caused me a lot of problems over the years. I take all the grief and store it on the inside. It's a peculiar thing – the symptom can be completely real but the cause might be completely psychosomatic. When you ask Clean questions about a symptom it gives you a way of exploring it and dealing with it very constructively. There is something about the way that you neither assume the truth about the situation nor question the sanity of person experiencing it that opens your mind to seeing what is actually happening.

Is there anything else?

It helps with my husband, Mike, actually. We have a habit of not really communicating very effectively and, because we've been together since Noah finished his ark, we think we know everything about each other. We start second-guessing one another, which can lead to assuming the worst. Then we end up being furious with each other! Being able to ask Clean questions helps us check out our assumptions so that we can stay together as co-parents through the storminess.

I'm much better at recognising other people's points of view now, which has been really important for me. It means that when I'm dealing with teachers and other care-givers, for example, I don't get anything like as uptight or cross as I used to because I appreciate that I don't know what they think and I don't know what it's like to be them. It feels much more gentle and helpful – like a 'loving kindness' place to be with it.

Harry

Harry is sixteen years old and in his GCSE[20] year at a large comprehensive school. He plays for a local football team at the weekends and dreams of becoming a sports physiotherapist one day. He can find the sheer volume of work that he's got to get through a bit overwhelming at times and there are a couple of teachers that he finds difficult to learn from. He came across Clean exploration on a module about 'learning

20. The General Certificate of Secondary Education (GCSE) is a qualification taken by pupils in the UK, usually at 16 years of age.

to learn' last year.

What impact has learning about Clean exploration had for you?

It's helped me understand myself better – I can delve deeper into the way I'm thinking and notice what's going on inside me more. For example, there were times I'd get into arguments. I'd feel my temperature rising and I'd get a surging feeling inside. Now I can notice when this is happening and press pause. It helps me stay more level-headed and gives me time to think about how other people might be seeing me.

I'm now better at taking a step back and challenging the way I'm seeing things, so I can get a different perspective on the situation. There's this teacher at school, for example, who doesn't listen to me or take on board what I'm saying. She used to make me so mad. Now I can see how I was in drama with her. I'd go straight into being a Victim because she seemed to have a grudge against me. I'd then go into Persecutor – thinking she was being really unreasonable and an awful teacher. I started to understand that she wasn't doing it on purpose, she just doesn't have the ability to listen in the way I want her to. When I try to put myself in her shoes it seems easier to accept her limitations. I still don't like the way she teaches but I feel calmer around her.

Anything else?

Yes. We did a Listening Space to find out more about what it means to be learning our best. I came up with this really cool metaphor that helped me understand why I learn more easily with some teachers than others.

I realised that when it's working well it's like I'm on a trapeze at the circus. I have to start slowly, with no sudden jolts of speed or gusts of wind. I don't mind if the trapeze speeds up as I become more able, but what's really important is that there's a safety net under the area we're working on to catch me if I fall – even though I can probably hold on myself and complete the task. The net could be something like receiving constructive criticism, having a chance to ask questions, or explaining things to other students who need help. It doesn't need to be completely cushioning – not everything needs to make sense or be totally OK – it just has to soften the fall.

I also realised that I need a chance to swing on the trapeze a bit and put things into practice before the teacher adds something else in. That isn't possible when they teach multiple things at once or if people ask more than one question at a time. Then I get confused because the progression is too rapid. I need the teacher to say, *'We'll come onto that in a minute.'* Or they could say, *'I'll explain that to you later'*, and go to the individual as opposed to explaining to the whole class.

This metaphor helped me understand and accept how things are for me. I might not be able to change the way they teach, but I can try and make sure I get a chance to get my questions answered, even if it's after the class. I now feel more in control when the gusts of wind come or the trapeze speeds up too quickly.

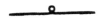

Karen

Karen has worked as a healthcare assistant in a small community outreach team for the past eight years. She works long days visiting patients in their homes and has found the increasing pressure on time for each visit both stressful and demoralising. She came across Clean questions at a workshop six months ago.

What impact has learning about Clean exploration had for you?

I'd been running around from visit to visit, juggling so many different balls, trying to stop them all from dropping. It was really upsetting me that we were being given less and less time with each patient. I didn't seem to have the time to get to know anyone properly.

Then I came across Clean questions. They seemed so simple I felt confident to give them a go straightaway. As soon as I made the conscious decision to listen Cleanly there was this kind of shift in me. I leant back slightly and become more relaxed, calmer. I could concentrate on what the other person had to say rather than thinking about what I was going to say next. I'd always thought I was a good listener but I don't think I'd realised just how much I was speaking for my patients, not giving them the space to talk. I started asking a few Clean questions here and there – just repeating back a few of their words and asking them a question – and they would tell me all sorts.

Just last week, for example, I was helping Mr Edwards get dressed and he said he liked the music that was playing on the radio. So I asked:

Is there anything else about liking that music?

Before, I would have carried on chatting about this or that. I wouldn't have picked up on what he'd said. But before I knew it he was telling me the most amazing stories about growing up in the War. I've never heard him talk like that before – and I've been visiting him for nearly three years now.

It's no longer me doing most of the talking, feeling I've got to have all the answers. These questions mean I switch off my usual chitter chatter and really listen. Odd really for something so simple, but it's made me become more curious about how things are for people rather than going into my usual busy fix-it mode. I have a different way to connect with people now.

Clean also helps me get to the nub of things more quickly when my patients bring up a problem – maybe a pain somewhere or something they're struggling with. I'll ask:

What kind of pain?
Whereabouts is that pain?
What kind of struggling?
Is there anything else about struggling?

It means they tell me what is happening for them rather than me second-guessing and assuming that I know. It always surprises me how many different answers there can be to these questions.

Clean listening has had a knock-on effect for how I feel about my job in general. I get more satisfaction because it feels like I'm connecting with people in a more meaningful way.

Amir

Amir has been teaching English at University for over 15 years. He has always been on the lookout for different ways to access the individuality within each student and went on a Clean Language course after reading a book about it.

What impact has learning about Clean exploration had for you?

One of the biggest differences for me has been in the way I respond to the things my students say when I raise a question or discussion point. I used to start a lot of questions with:

> *Tell me about this…*
> or
> *I'd like to know more about that…*

I was always bringing myself into it. I now hone in on certain words in their answers or comments, repeat them back and ask things like:

> **Is there anything else about** that?
> or
> **What kind of** [whatever they've just said]?

It really works – it helps them further develop their thoughts and encourages more reflective thinking.

Yesterday, for example, we were talking about success and I just echoed back some of their words and asked a few Clean questions, which gave them space to examine in their own heads what they meant by the things they'd said. It made it about them rather than me. By repeating back I'm inviting them to examine the words they've chosen more closely. So, if a student comes to me and says:

This paragraph of my work is not very good.

Even if I agree that it's not good, I don't say:

Yes, it's not very good.

Instead I'll respond with:

Is there anything else about not very good?

Rather than having me analyse it and assume what they mean, they have to think for themselves and decide what *'not very good'* means to them. The responsibility is handed back to them and it means I do less telling or explaining.

Of course I don't use Clean all the time but, when I do, I notice that I'm not rescuing them with advice and ideas as much as I used to. It seems to encourage them to generate their own possibilities.

Although I've always felt quite confident in my role as a teacher and have tried to make my teaching quite student-centred, I don't think I'd been making people so responsible for themselves in the past. So much of our work is collaborative these days and it's easy for some students to just drift or coast in a group situation. Since Clean is all about the individual, it gives them more importance or significance. I'm able to ask about a uniqueness that can only come from the answers that they give. I think it makes them feel more listened to but it also enables me to challenge each one of them in their thinking so they can't just drift.

For the students who are just cruising, it's like they're a light with the dimmer switch turned down low or a computer on snooze mode. When I ask Clean questions it becomes about them and not anybody else, so they have to turn their light up to a brighter setting for a while and shine out a bit more. It seems to help them find their inner core or inner strength, especially when we're talking about ideas where there is no right or wrong answer. It gives everybody in the class the chance to shine a bit more.

Is there anything else?

I've always found metaphor fascinating, but now I use Clean to encourage students to discover their own metaphors. At the beginning of a 12-week course earlier this year I asked my students to explore how they would like the course to be and how they would like to be. They seemed to generate metaphors very easily. One person wanted to be like an eagle soaring in the sky, another was like a horse free to roam around the field, and so on. They asked Clean questions of one another to expand on their answers.

We kept reflecting back to those metaphors throughout the

course, with me saying things like:

How is that eagle?
  or
What's happened to that horse?

It gave them something tangible to latch on to, to describe their experience.

With another group, I wanted them to explore their experience of the project they had just started working on. I brought in a whole range of images – there were pictures of roads, boats on the sea, rock climbers, all sorts of things. I asked them to choose an image that represents what it was like for them now. I wanted them to connect with the way they were seeing themselves. They asked each other Clean questions to explore what it was that the image represented for them. There was a real buzz to the room. People were coming up with all sorts of insights about things that were working well for them, things that would work better.

Anything else?

I can also see just how useful a Listening Space would be in tutorials where students come and they're not quite sure what they want to talk about. You could tell them that you're going to set 15 minutes aside, and explain the process to them, starting with the question, *'What would you like to explore?'*

They might want to talk about something that's not even to do with their academic work: it might be to do with homesickness or the way they manage their time. But it would be good to give them a space to be listened to by their tutor. It would give the tutor some structure to explore the challenges that the student might be facing. You don't risk going into drama with them – wanting to rescue them or getting frustrated with them because they can't see the things that seem obvious to you. Having the explanation at the beginning makes the boundaries and rules really clear and understandable and lets everyone know what to expect.

Anything else?

I've noticed that Clean also helps me reflect for myself. For example, I'll take time to think about what I'm like when I'm teaching or listening at my best and I ask myself Clean questions again and again. I become curious about my answers rather than seeing it as a criticism of myself, which has made me more open to change. It makes me more excited about my own capacity and capabilities.

Jo

Jo is a police sergeant with 15 years' experience in the force. She manages a community policing team of 16 people, spread over a wide geographical area. The demands of her role have changed significantly over the past couple of years, resulting in *'an increasing number of jobs half finished'* – which she finds very stressful. Whilst many of these changes are beyond her control, she feels that her stress levels aren't helped by the fact that she is *'not a good closer'*. She came across Clean questions at a training event about communication.

What impact has learning about Clean exploration had for you?

I learnt about Clean questions at a workshop a while ago and did a Listening Space with a colleague. We ended up talking about managing sickness in some of the staff on my team. It helped me realise that I need to have more structure to the conversations I was having with those staff members who were off sick about how we could work together to get them back to work. I needed to be more structured about always bringing them back to the reason for me being there when I went to see them.

It's like there are two levels of tethering post needed. First, I need to let the person talk around the issue from their perspective. I was already using a mix of echoing back and various open questions. But learning about Clean questions has helped me become more aware of the fact that I was going in to these conversations with assumptions about how things were for them and I probably had too strong a desire to rescue them. I wasn't really giving them the opportunity to speak for themselves.

Second, I need to put my own tethering post in place around the conversation. This post is about making sure that we leave with some kind of agreed plan at the end of it. However, formulating a plan that is going to work for both of us can only happen once they've had a chance to graze around the problem sufficiently. My level is built on the level they've given.

This realisation has had a knock on effect for other areas of my work, which is mainly communities' work. Some of the neighbour disputes that we get called into can be particularly challenging to manage. Much of the time we're dealing with creating long-term solutions for ongoing problems. People come to us with a long list of complaints about their neighbours – someone parking in their space, the loud music next door, a neighbour who keeps staring at them, a dog that keeps fouling the garden. There may be ten years of problems given to us all in one go, not in chronological order, going off at tangents at various points – issues that are clearly causing real distress for the person.

It's easy to end up in rescuer role because they will look to me to help them. But in ninety-nine percent of neighbour disputes they have the answers themselves. Invariably, the best solutions are the ones they've come up with themselves rather than those I might suggest. If they come up with their own plan then they're more likely to follow it. If I tell them the plan, chances are they won't follow it and they'll keep coming back to me to ask, *'What do you want me to do now?'*

The Listening Space helped me bring more structure to separating out each issue the person raises. I'll usually start by giving a summary of the background history that we already know about to help us get to the point:

I'm aware that…

I'll then ask:

So where are we now?
    or
What's the current state of play?

I can then create a separate tethering post for each of the issues that they raise. I'll echo back and ask some Clean questions, giving them a chance to graze and explore the problem. I now make sure that I bring them back to that particular tethering post until we've got an agreed action plan before moving on to the next issue. It encourages them to find a solution that is a best fit for them.

If they mention other problems, we'll put them to one side until we've bottomed out the first issue and decided who is doing what. Since I'm not going in to rescue in the same way, I can be clearer on separating out whether the issue is a police matter or not and whether they need to be signposted to other agencies. It makes it easier to manage expectations and I'm less at risk of overpromising on the support that I can offer.

I'm now getting closure on one issue at a time as opposed to trying to deal with the whole thing in one go. I'll round up each issue by saying:

> *We've discussed this, this is what we've planned, this is what you're going to do, and this is what we will do.*
> *Are you happy with that?*

I'll then send them a letter reminding them of what we've discussed. It means they are less at risk of developing that constant attachment to me. If you don't get closure on each of the issues, you know that person is going to come back sooner or later and ask for help again – whether that's six weeks or six months from now. Whether it's for managing sickness or for neighbourhoods, they've got to do their own grazing in order for us to get an agreed plan that they'll follow. They need to come up with their solution to the issue and to stick with it, otherwise everyone's dissatisfied.

I'm finding that now I don't have those lingering jobs that aren't resolved. I haven't got that constant feeling of juggling several balls at once, knowing that I'm bound to drop one of them at some point because I've left things unresolved.

Andy

Andy is a fifty-two year old composer and lecturer at one of the Royal Music Colleges. Students often come to him because they are stuck in the piece they are working on – it's a feeling he knows only too well himself! He was introduced to Clean questions by a friend and fellow musician who uses them in his one-to-one music teaching practice.

What impact has learning about Clean exploration had for you?

There are so many different levels to using Clean questions. I might use them in a conversational way to find out whether I've understood what one of my students has said:

I'm feeling overwhelmed.
Is there anything else about feeling overwhelmed?

Or I might use them to help students who are stuck and searching for inspiration. Some of them feel they need inspiration before they will strike a note, but waiting doesn't work – inspiration is an industrial process. Clean questions help them explore their ideas and get the creative process going – whether they are struggling to get started or stuck in a piece and not sure where they are going. We stick a tethering post in the ground for whatever issue they want to explore to help keep things more focussed.

I've also got a friend who facilitates me in developing my ideas when I'm stuck with my own composing. Usually when I'm commissioned to compose a piece, they just give the parameters for the performance – how long it will be, what instruments will be performing – but they don't give a topic. Being 'in the lighthouse' and doing a Listening Space is great for exploration of that initial conception because it's so generative. The creative spark becomes the tethering post and you can graze around as your ideas form. In a lot of ways the composition is itself mindful exploration.

For me, structured music works better when it has a narrative, a story to tell. Having a tethering post helps to make sure that the piece I'm composing holds this narrative and gives it a consistency and an internal logic. Yes, you can move quite a long way from the post, but you never lose sight of it. The listener might not be explicitly aware that this is happening but holding the narrative makes the piece work better.

There is also something about a Listening Space that helps me connect with what's important to me, with the things that make me authentically me. It's probably because the exploration is so embodied. For me, being authentic is about accepting who you are and being proud of it. When you can have compassion for yourself in this way it seems to enable kindness towards others. Authenticity is also probably the most important part of the creative process – and the most intangible. That's where metaphor can be so helpful: hope becomes a torch that you carry with you to see into the dark, for example.

I've actually sorted out quite a lot thanks to Clean!

Is there anything else?

Clean questions come into their own with a group collaborative process. For example, talking about musical detail to a visual artist doesn't necessarily work well. Dynamics, tonality, texture, timbre – all these concepts have different meanings to the different art forms. So 'dynamics' will mean one thing to a choreographer and something else to a musician. Clean questions help you to become clearer about what the other person is saying and to find a common language for what you want to express through metaphor. They give people a way of getting curious about one another.[21]

Thinking back on it, I wish I'd known about these questions a few years ago when I did some collaborative work between a theatre company and a cinematographer. It's very difficult to have a completely equal collaboration between art forms – one usually takes precedence over the other. Generally music is a thing that contextualises image, so if you go and see a silent film, the music accompanies it and enhances it. Often as composers we end up coming in at the last five minutes, having to do a bit

---

21. Caitlin Walker gives some lovely examples of this in her book. (2014). *From Contempt to Curiosity: Creating Conditions for Groups to Collaborate Using Clean Language and Systemic Modelling*. Porchester: Clean Publishing.

of music to something that already exists. But as a collaborator it's much more satisfying to be in there at the beginning, helping conceive the idea.

I was there at the first discussion between the contemporary theatre performance practitioners, who like working with rather vague ideas about how the narrative should go, and a cinematographer, who has very specific ideas of what things should look like. And then there's me, wondering what does 'white box' mean in music? Those initial discussions were interesting but a bit frustrating. If I'd used Clean questions I know I'd have been able to get much more understanding of what they were actually describing and I could have avoided the frustration. It's difficult to get a purchase on descriptions of abstract images when you don't think in that way yourself. I think a Listening Space would have helped us to explore the core idea at a much more fundamental level when it was launched and there would have been a greater sense of integrity to the project as a whole. As it was, I didn't have the right way of communicating with them and I couldn't be more involved beyond the initial discussions, until I was called in much nearer the end.

Amara

Amara is a social researcher. A key part of her job involves interviewing people to find out more about their experience of their situation. In order for her results to be trustworthy, she needs to be able to gain access to other people's perspectives. A colleague told her about the way in which Clean questions help to keep your assumptions out of the way when you interview people. So, eighteen months ago she decided to attend a Clean interviewing course.

What impact has learning about Clean exploration had for you?

I'd been a researcher for about four years before coming across Clean Language. After attending the Clean interviewing course, I started a new project researching people's experiences of anxiety and depression – how it affects them, the challenges they face. We're trying to find out more about the support these people feel they need from their employers to be able to return to work successfully. This kind of research is all about trying to get to the bottom of how the people we interview are experiencing things. Otherwise we end up making suggestions based on our idea of what it's like to have anxiety or depression, not theirs.

Learning about Clean questions was a real light-bulb moment for me. I was a bit shocked when I realised just how differently we interpret the words people use! I'd thought I was good at asking questions in an unbiased way, but it made me realise that my questions were riddled with 'hidden' assumptions. Even a seemingly open question, *'How would you explain your situation to another person?'*, can influence the way someone responds. They might subtly alter what they say to provide a more socially acceptable response – something that another person would want to hear.

The thing with Clean questions is that I know that it's all about the interviewee. Repeating back means I don't even change the words they have chosen. Since the credibility of my research is dependent on trying not to contaminate what the interviewees tell me with the meaning I'm giving to it, taking a Clean approach seemed the obvious thing to do.

I soon realised that Clean questions can quickly get to the heart of the matter in a way that often surprises people. Just yesterday one interviewee said to me, *'I kind of knew these things, but your questions have helped me reflect on my situation very differently.'*

I was also very excited about being able to bring the structure of the Listening Space into the way I interviewed. Obviously I can't just start the exploration with the usual question, *'What would you like to explore?'*, because I'm wanting to find out about a specific thing – their experience of anxiety and depression, in this instance. So what I do is invite them into a particular field to graze – the 'research' field. This creates a boundary to the exploration. I'll start by saying, *'Tell me about your experience of anxiety'* (or whatever the topic in question is).

I then have a choice of tethering post:

- The research topic itself, or
- An embodied word that they have used in their answer.

This structure helps to keep them on topic. I noticed that I was getting more information in a shorter space of time. We normally set aside an hour for each interview, but within 15 to 20 minutes I've got a whole lot of rich information. I've then got time to invite them into a neighbouring research field and establish a new tethering post to explore a different aspect of their experience if I want to.

I did find using a Clean approach difficult at first – a bit scary even – because I had to let go of the control I had around the questions. Although there is real structure to the process, once the interviewee starts talking they choose which direction they are going to graze next – you just follow on your next question from what they have just said, bringing them back to the tethering post each time, until they are done grazing or you are out of time. But once I'd got over that fear, it actually made the whole interview much easier to conduct.

Over to You

I hope you have enjoyed reading the stories that Sophie, Harry, Karen, Amir, Jo, Andy and Amara have shared with us. Time and again people tell me of the positive impact that using this simple tool has had for them – repeating back a person's words and using Clean questions, along with a mindset of curiosity. When we are listened to Cleanly we feel heard in a way that can be very liberating. We often find that when we are given the space for Clean exploration, as if from nowhere, a metaphor comes to life, bringing an almost magical quality to our thinking.

Some of you may already be using the Listening Space for exploration and want to experiment with bringing this way of listening into new areas of your work or personal life.

Others of you will be using Clean questions in general conversation and want to see what happens when you start using the Listening Space with others for more in-depth exploration.

And there will be others who are totally new to Clean. If this is the case, just remember that it only takes one small step to get going. Just press pause, get curious and ask yourself, *What Clean question could I ask of someone today?* Before long you will find yourself repeating words back and dropping these questions into everyday conversations automatically. You will start to become curious about people in a different way, in particular the metaphors that they naturally use to describe their experience. With practice you'll soon gain the confidence to create a Listening Space for others, giving them the freedom to explore their own thoughts and emotions, helping them get to the nub of things in a very creative way.

As someone once said to me:

The simplicity and directness of these questions seems to cut through all the overlay of thoughts – those 'shoulds and shouldn'ts', the expectations and over-analysis. They neither suggest nor get in the way, and help me to get curious about my emotions. Metaphors seem to arise naturally – I can't really explain why. Images just spring up, and these metaphors become a comfortable and creative way of connecting with my authentic self.

It is my belief that listening and asking questions in this way is perhaps the greatest gift that we can give to ourselves and to others.

Dear Explorer,

I hope you've enjoyed your journey through this Lighthouse of Mindful Exploration.

I'm really interested in hearing about how using Clean questions and the Listening Space have helped you in your life.

If you have your own stories that you would like to share with me then I'd love to hear from you. You can leave me a message in one of the following ways:

- Website – www.thelisteningspace.co.uk
- Facebook page – www.facebook.com/listeningspace
- Instagram – www.instagram.com/the_listening_space
- Twitter – www.twitter.com/listeningspace2
- YouTube channel – The Listening Space

And if you would like to be supported in learning The Listening Space process, then you might like to join a Listening Space course – *www.thelisteningspace.co.uk/ courses*.

Happy exploring!
Tamsin

Further Reading

If you have enjoyed the exploration you have done through metaphor, then you might like to learn more about the various ways that Clean Language is being used:

Further reading about Clean Language

Dunbar, A. (2017). *Clean Coaching: The Insider Guide to Making Change Happen*. Abingdon: Routledge.

Harland, P. (2009). *The Power of Six*. London: Wayfarer Press.

Harland, P. (2012). *Trust Me, I'm the Patient*. London: Wayfarer Press.

Lawley, J. and Tompkins, P. (2000). *Metaphors in Mind: Transformation through Symbolic Modelling:* Lawley. The Developing Company Press.

McCracken, J. (2016). *Clean Language in the Classroom*. Carmarthen: Crown House Publishing Ltd.

Pole, N. (2017). *Words that Touch: How to Ask Questions Your Body Can Answer*. London: Singing Dragon.

Sullivan, W. and Rees, J. (2008). *Clean Language; Revealing Metaphors and Opening Minds*. Carmarthen: Crown House Publishing Ltd.

Walker, C. (2014). *From Contempt to Curiosity: Creating Conditions for Groups to Collaborate using Clean Language and Systemic Modelling*. Portchester: Clean Publishing.

Way, M. (2013). *Clean Approaches for Coaches: How to Create the Conditions for Change Using Clean Language and Symbolic Modelling*. Portchester: Clean Publishing.

There are also some useful websites to visit:
www.cleanlearning.co.uk
www.trainingattention.co.uk
www.cleanlanguage.co.uk
www.cleanchange.co.uk
www.cleancoaching.com

For further reading about mindfulness:

Kabat-Zinn, J. (1990). *Full Catastrophe Living: How To Cope With Stress, Pain and Illness Using Mindfulness Meditation*. London: Piatkus.

Kabat-Zinn, J. (1994). *Wherever You Go, There You Are: Mindfulness Meditation for Everyday Life*. London: Piatkus.

Wax, R. (2013). *Sane New World: Taming the Mind*. London: Hodder and Stoughton.

Williams, M., and Penman, D. (2011). *Mindfulness: a Practical Guide to Finding Peace in a Frantic World*. London: Piatkus.

Index

Acknowledgements

I have many people to thank for making this book possible:

My father – for showing me the importance of asking questions and being curious.

My mother – for encouraging me to find joy in creative expression.

David Grove – for giving us the gift of Clean Language; a method of enquiry that is both respectful and highly creative.

Wendy Sullivan, Penny Tompkins, James Lawley, Caitlin Walker and Marian Way – who have inspired me through their teaching of Clean Language.

Sue Sharp and Emily Walker – for our playful exploration of the ways in which we can bring Clean Language into our everyday lives.

John De Simone – whose intellect, intuition and willingness to experiment helped bring the Listening Space into existence.

To all the clients, fellow explorers, and people who have attended the various Listening Space courses and workshops that I have run over the past three years – and helped me shape the Listening Space process into its current form.

The seven individuals in the final chapter – who have been so generous in sharing their stories about the impact that Clean exploration has had on their lives.

Elizabeth Davis, Ina James, Lucinda Whitehead, Fiona Waddington, Alison Blackler, John Gallagher, Doris Stahl, Kate Smith, Jane Clappison and Karon Rickatson – for their support and encouragement, especially when self-doubt came knocking at my door!

My sister Marieke Wrigley – for introducing me to mindfulness and helping me clarify the connections between mindfulness and Clean exploration.

Sue Sharp, Elizabeth Davis, Anna Connell, John Gallagher, Juliet Mackney, Paul Waddington, Emily De Simone, Anna Heddle, Karon Rickatson, Mohammed Karolia, Ina James, Mary Cutland and my father – who gave me invaluable feedback for the first edition of this book. And to Lorna Reid, Ruth Huckle, Emily De Simone, David O'Sullivan, Joanne Rule and Julia Pakora for their comments and suggestions for this second edition.

Lucy Monkman – who brought the characters in my book to life with her wonderful illustrations. I can't tell you how excited I felt when she first brought me face-to-face with my tethered goat!

Nick Machen – for making the Lighthouse of Mindful Exploration look so inviting with his cover design.

Adele Kelly – for creating a layout to the book which I find so clean and clear. Her patience with my endless 'editorial tweaking' has been impressive, to say the least!

Siân-Elin Flint-Freel, my editor and writing mentor – who helped me to find my own voice in writing this book. I am quite certain that I wouldn't have got this far without her ongoing encouragement and expertise.

And finally, my family – who are a constant reminder that a Clean mindset helps me to see the amazingness in the people that they are.

About the Author

Tamsin Hartley, MSc, worked as a physiotherapist for ten years before taking time out to bring up her young family. She then retrained to work as a coach, trainer and workshop facilitator. She has always been drawn to using metaphor in her work, and when a friend introduced her to Clean Language it wasn't long before she was hooked. Here was a respectful way of working with people's metaphors that is both resourceful and richly creative.

Tamsin has combined the principles of mindful awareness with exploration using Clean Language to create the Listening Space – a new approach to listening to yourself and others that can help transform your life.

She published a second book in 2019, *Captured Moments: Poems Inspired by A Listening Space*, a collection that resulted from various Listening Space sessions. The book includes an activity that invites the reader to explore their own experience through metaphor with the use of Clean questions.

She lives with her family in East Yorkshire.

Lightning Source UK Ltd.
Milton Keynes UK
UKHW021820050521
383163UK00007B/220

9 780995 785427